MEN IN SANDALS

MEN
IN SANDALS

FATHER RICHARD MADDEN, O.C.D.
HOLY HILL, WISCONSIN

THE BRUCE PUBLISHING COMPANY
MILWAUKEE

Imprimi Potest:
      THOMAS KILDUFF, O.C.D.
      Provincial

Nihil Obstat:
      JOHN A. SCHULIEN, S.T.D.
      Censor librorum

Imprimatur:
      ✠ ALBERT G. MEYER
      Archiepiscopus Milwauchiensis

17a Septembris 1954

Catholic University of America Classification Number: 271.73

Library of Congress Catalog Card Number: 54–12550

To

my mother and dad,
who, in giving me life,
gave me the chance to become
a priest; and in honor of Mary,
Queen Beauty of Carmel

Three years ago Father Francis A. Barry, then Director of Vocations in the Archdiocese of Boston, said, "If you want an increase of vocations in your Order, write a book."

This is the book.

Acknowledgments

THE writer would like to extend the highest possible measure of gratitude and appreciation to Margaret Madden Maschi, my devoted cousin who, with the eye of a humorist, saw us as we appear, and with the eye of an artist saw us as we are, and produced, at the price of much time and effort, the original sketches and jacket for this book; and to her husband, Pete, who co-operated in the work by doing with his heart what he could not do with his pen; to Irma Jakus and Judy Rieger for the time they so willingly gave to the correcting and typing of the manuscript; and to all my fellow Carmelites, whose Christlike charity and priceless friendship, have made me ever proud to be numbered among the "men in sandals."

Introduction

THIS, to put it bluntly, is a book about Discalced Carmelites. I write about them because, although people are interesting, Discalced Carmelites are more interesting than people. I write about them, too, because I know more about this subject that I know about any other.

This book is not an analysis of their sanctity. It is not an insight into the deep recesses of their spiritual life. Nor can it, in any way, be classified as Carmelite literature because it falls far short of the high standards set by our holy parents, St. Teresa of Avila and St. John of the Cross. This book is simply an effort to convey the fact that, although religious life may not always be easy, there is nothing quite so satisfying. It is not a dreary thing. It is not a world wherein somber, brown-robed men straggle through dingy vaulted corridors. It is not a life of long faces and sad hearts. Rather, it is a kingdom that rarely feels the draughts of true sorrow. Lived with, and in imitation of Christ, it could only be, even in its essence, a life of honest joy. So this is a book about Discalced Carmelites — although it should be made quite clear that the opinions and views herein expressed are not necessarily those of my superiors or fellow religious.

Further, I do not think that I take undue liberties

by including within the scope of these pages all priests, of all Orders and all dioceses, who by the fullest possible dedication of their lives to God, have sacrificed their green years that the years of others might be ever greener. For if there is such a thing as heroism in our day, these men possess it. One of the most extraordinary phenomena of our times is that monasteries, rather than being filled with angels, are really filled with men. Angels have come by their holiness without effort; but fallen men have come by theirs through great effort and much sacrifice. For holiness is not only a state of being. It is also the result of a man's endless struggle, his constant plodding, his groveling, sometimes, across the span of a single lifetime.

Some of these men live in big houses; others live in small ones. But the little Carmelite cell, where breezes refuse to stir, where in summer a friar knows full well the meaning of heat, where even spiders spurn to dwell — this is where I live. It is here where I work, study, and pray. It is here where I write this book. It is my home, and I like it.

The ancient monks of Mount Carmel lived in caves. We gave that up years ago. But the present cell still retains all the requisite and basic simplicity of the eremitical life. It is, in short, nothing to sing songs about. The cell itself, measuring about eight by twelve feet, is not much for running marathons in, but it is certainly no problem to keep clean. The furnishings are almost nil. The bed consists of a thin mattress spread on a wooden plank which has a devilish knack of detaching itself in the middle of the night from the two wooden horses supporting it. A bookcase holds the wisdom of the ages. There is a table with drawers that stick; and upon the wall hangs a plain wooden cross which keeps us in mind of the God-Man who made us what we are. Then as an added smack of luxury there is a wardrobe closet set against the wall, which adequately provides for the clothing of short men, but which leaves my own pants all wrinkled and crumpled at the bottom.

It is not much as far as living quarters go, but a man certainly grows up to it. A visitor once remarked, "Living in here is like doing time." But a man who "does time" has lost his freedom. We have found it. In the prison of our tiny cells we have found Christ. As long as He is there, every stream flows by our door and every star shines through our window. The world which we have left, the best part of it, with all its beauty and tranquillity, all its freedom and expansiveness — everything has come with Christ and with all this we have been fenced in. Small wonder we are free.

And God knows that, for all their poverty and simplicity, our cells are a comparative haven. For upon our walls cannot be found the cold, glistening blobs of water that clung to the walls of a stable in Bethlehem. Nor can there be found on our walls the blood that stained the walls of Carmelite cells in Spain. And the bombs which razed the walls of Carmelite monasteries in England and Germany have never even come close to ours.

The walls still stand, quite buff and drab; but strong in security. They have looked down on many men before me. If they could, they might tell a long thrilling story of the silent greatness which comes from living and working unseen. They have enclosed the virtue and goodness of weak men who hung their capes here. They have funneled to heaven the prayers of weary workers for God. Their glory is a muted one.

They fence me in but it is good to dwell with peace. It is good to live with the silence that makes one think about the really important things in life. It is consoling to know that evil has difficulty entering here.

Yes, this is where I live — in a small room that has never seen a cushioned chair nor felt the balm of beautiful music; in a cubicle where the alarm clock is silenced in the dark each morning by a long, searching foot; where there is no place to hide from the eyes of God. It is a confinement in freedom. It is an open imprisonment. For God is here, and with God we possess the world. Ours are the things which we shall never see from our window. We walk every road, climb every hill, sail every sea; for God is all this and He is here.

My cell is my eight-by-twelve kingdom where dust gathers in little ripples across the floor. It is not big. It is not luxurious. It is not comfortable. But the things it is not are of little consequence. The important thing is *what it is*. It is my home.

Contents

Priesthood

Novitiate Days

❧ I ❧

The Way In

ANY man who sits down to write a book for the first time is really up against it. How does he do it? Presuming (*a*) that he has the material for the book and (*b*) that he knows his subject, how does he go about expressing himself in such a way as to avoid making a fool of himself? And being a priest as well as a religious, having tasted fully all the hard things, the bitterness, the loneliness of the religious life, how can he begin to convince the world that this is the greatest life of them all?

The problem here is to *convince*. Those who serve mammon have called us mad. And they have reasons. Even those who serve God, questioning either our motives or our sanity, have asked, "Whatever made you do it? What is wrong with the world?" To these questions and to these people who ask them of us, we have no answer. We converse on different levels. We are poles apart. And even if, all things being equal, we took them aside for a few private words, we still would not reach them. We would not convince them. And we ourselves would probably end up by shrugging our shoulders, shaking our heads, and saying nothing.

Religious life, like the God who sustains it, is a

3

mystery. Maybe this explains why we are able to draw so much happiness from it. All we know is that by throwing in our lot with God we have found nothing wanting; while those who try everything else *but* God, are still lost. They still wander as orphans upon the face of the earth. They are still hungry.

Furthermore, what does a machinist or a doctor or a lawyer care what a friar thinks or feels? What does a typist in an insurance office care about what time we get up in the morning? And if there is no common denominator, no basic tie that unites us, what is the reason for a book at all?

So, as I say, the man who sits down to write a book for the first time is really up against it. Especially, if he is a Discalced Carmelite. Therefore, with a hope that at least someone will be interested in reading what I might have to say, I begin at the beginning.

It all started on the day when three of us stood together before the large bleak door of a Carmelite monastery, holding brand new suitcases in our hands, inhaling as free men our last draughts of sweet air. But somehow nothing fitted. No logical reason existed for our presence there. No single person was responsible. No single event or experience. It must have been the combination of many people and many things that set three kids imagining they had the guts and the power to make priests of themselves.

We were just out of high school, "bigdomes" by virtue of our diplomas, and still retaining the memory of our valedictorian's screaming, "Now we must go out to make our ways in the hard, cruel world" with about the same emphasis that he would say, "Now we must go out and jump off some high bridge." We had one thing in common — we were from the same parish, the Immaculate Conception in Germantown, a section of Philadelphia that has seen its day. Our parish in the fifty years of its existence had given a few over 250 boys and girls to the church — a pretty good record. So maybe just by living there we came by a vocation automatically. This might account for part of it.

We might also attribute part of our vocation to the Vincentian Fathers who were our parish priests. Always having been men worthy of imitation, they must have inspired many boys to think about the priesthood. Maybe we got our call serving their Masses, working around their rectory, taking occasional furtive detours through their dining room, hoisting peppermints from their table as we went. Maybe we got it from Father Campbell, the great priest who had while there ridden herd on two hundred altar boys; and who has probably found in death that he was as dearly loved by as many boys as Father Flanagan was.

And because teaching Sisters are so instrumental in fostering vocations, maybe we got the idea while under the tutelage of the Immaculate Heart Sisters, and specifically, the Sister who taught the eighth grade, Sister Anne Madeleine, the beacon, the woman who was truly a boy's nun, who was loved beyond her highest realization, and who molded boys' lives with the same perfection and thoroughness with which she taught grammar.

All these were possibilities, if we were interested in

possibilities. But we weren't. So nothing added up as we stood before the entrance of Carmel. There was no explanation that we knew of. Why should a kid do it? Why should he leave a world he loved? Personally, I never had any ax to grind with the world or with the people who lived in it. I rather liked the setup. I didn't enjoy saying good-by to my folks, because I came from one of the world's greatest homes, with parents who found out that in having eight sons life was more interesting, however hectic, than it might have been in having one; and who have discovered in their advancing years that they have no regrets to haunt them, no fears for ever having attempted to usurp the right of God, who alone has the power to say who should be born and who should not — and when. So quite possibly, home had a lot to do with making me a priest. My brothers always paired off for their brawls leaving me to referee, a situation of which I soon became weary until I decided to go out and find my own brawls — with the souls of men.

Finally, three of us left the old parish, clambered aboard a train, and one thousand miles later were dropped off before this strange doorway in this lonely spot. Waifs we were, cut off from our homes, not yet taken into our monastery, floating on a bubble of doubt which threatened to burst at any minute and to cast us into the depths below.

Frankly, there was no lilting joy in my heart. Fear would be a better word. Fear that I might bungle the whole thing. Fear that I might succeed and spend the rest of my life in a cloister. These are the times when you wish for a fleeting moment that God had let you alone, that He had given the vocation to somebody else. Anybody but you.

Storybooks tell us about men who gave themselves to God by rushing through the monastery and flinging themselves upon the chapel floor, all the while weeping copious tears of joy for having come. Not me! It wasn't going to be like that with me. I wasn't going to do any flinging. Nor was I going to glide up to the tabernacle and whisper, "O God, You lucky person You, here I am." I was just going to be led. Nothing more. And if they led me into the coalbin and left me standing there, there I would stand. No, my entrance into monastic life did not have in it the slightest element of "coming home." It was too grim for that. Nobody can be joyous when he feels a vise crushing his innards. That explains why, on the day of admission into the Order, I seemed to have forsaken my sense of humor. I had sacrificed laughter. I was miserable.

However, there was one point the three of us had to get straight before we rang that bell. The life which we were about to tackle was a good one. Discontent could possibly arise in a monastery. But actually, if any dissonance ever sprang up between a man and his religious life, it was the man's fault, not the life's. The life would always be right; a man could easily be wrong. So if we expected to find that good which religious life promised, we would have to face up to it and live it. The Rule would satisfy us if we followed it; it would break us if we didn't.

Convinced finally that now was the time to make

history, we shuffled up to the door and leaned on the
buzzer. Nothing happened. Then and there we were
initiated into the great truth that nobody in a monastery
is ever in a hurry to answer the door. So as all people
must, we waited. We had no intention of ringing a
second time. If no one answered the door after that
first summons, we would streak down the road and go
back home (which seemed to be a pretty good idea at
the moment). But before we could make our getaway,
the door opened. Maybe it was only an illusion, but
there before us stood a large brown spider that seemed
to say, "Come into my den, little flies." We went in.
The door clicked shut behind us.

Looking back on that unique day, trying to recapture
the emotion, the impact, and the incomprehensible sense
of depression that rode my back, only serves to make
the incident even more vague than it was at the time.
The Novice Master was just too patronizing. Too kind.
He fluttered around us, inquired if we had had a comfortable trip, told us what wonderful Carmelites we
were going to make — then took us down to the refectory, where he arranged for some scrambled eggs. I,
fresh from the outside, with the strains of Glenn Miller's
String of Pearls still in my ears, and on my tongue the
futile taste of my last steak, felt no more like eating
then, there, or that, than I felt like swimming the
Channel.

Then to our rooms. One by one we wheeled out of
formation as we came to our assigned cells, saying good-
by to one another with our eyes and coming at last to
the worst moment of them all. For this was the time

when the thing really hit, when it clawed deeply into my stomach and rested there like a hot, burning coal. I took in the cell — a plank bed, a table and chair, a pasteboard closet buckled at the middle, a Bible, and the *Autobiography of the Little Flower.*

All this I had expected. But the one thing for which I was totally unprepared was the big, yellow pear plunked down in the middle of the table. A pear! Good Lord, of all things, a pear! Yet, strangely in all its incongruity, it lay there like a wedge of light cut away from the darkness. The master had put it there. Maybe the old boy wasn't so bad after all. Maybe he understood our feelings. Maybe he was human, and in an effort to tide us over the raw spot, in an effort to lighten our burden, he offered us the only luxury he could. He gave abundantly of his poverty. With all the deftness he possessed he had evidently tried to say with this gift, "You have picked a hard row to hoe. But life is still fun. We may take your freedom, your heart, and your mind for God; we may close you up in a little room, smother you with a roof, bind your hands, shackle your feet; but we will never take away your right to sit down on the pinnacle of your Gethsemani, and sip the sweet nectar of a juicy pear." So I sipped.

Still the quiet reigned. Silence hung in thick folds throughout the house. If there were noises, they were muffled. But suddenly came the sound of voices, the soft distant chanting of the friars. The *Salve Regina.* Everything else at that moment might have been ugly but that was beautiful. That was really beautiful. You just didn't hear stuff like that on the outside. Nobody ever sang like that back in Germantown. Maybe this was a sign of better days. So sit there and listen. Take it all in. Sit there on that crummy hard bed and let it carry you away. Let it break your heart with its loveliness. Let it lift you, boy — it's all you've got left!

So that was it. The first night behind the walls. There was nothing to do. Nothing happened. I just sat there and stared like a zombi, while homesickness, like thick cold molasses, slid over my head and crawled down my body, leaving me weak and rubbery. And only after becoming aware that I would be much happier asleep than I was awake, I clutched my rosary and climbed into bed. But I never knew as I fell asleep, that if I was in bad shape that night, it was the last time. For from then on I would never again know the meaning of blackness, loneliness, or fear. God would see to that. So would the men around me.

❧ II ❧

This Thing Called Sleep

WHEN you sleep in a monastery, you've got to sleep fast because they don't give you very much time to do it. And so, when the long hand had made a series of hurried circuits around the clock's face, I arose at the morning summons and threw myself into the business of religious life. But that was the first and the last morning that I ever got out of bed with any sort of relish. At the moment, however, life became the horse of another color and all the shadows of the night had vanished. Feeling as I did, I was greatly disedified at the sight of veteran novices going to morning choir with no apparent interest in monastic life.

The reason for my attitude was obvious. I had become a victim of novelty. This novelty can be defined as a gift, sent by God to a new novice, for the purpose of deadening any pain that might otherwise come from his first buffetings at the hands of superiors. Novelty is the state of mind that makes a new novice shed tears during mental prayer, giving him to believe that he is already in the upper mansions of St. Teresa's interior castle. It is that which brings him to don and doff his holy habit with passionate delight, makes him volunteer for dirty jobs — changes him, in short, from a man of the

11

world into a contemplative of Christ. To an old novice, this trait is disgusting. But for the new one it is a wonderful thing to have around.

If I said that novelty wears off, I would not be making any world-shattering statement. Because it does. And this I found out all too soon, especially when it came to getting out of bed in the morning or in the middle of the night. I discovered to my eventual sorrow that monasticism is not a drawn-out spiritual orgy. Humanly speaking, no man in religious life can be perpetually thrilled. His vocation does not engender a constant tingling in his body. Comes the day when he must bow his head to the truth that any life, lived after the manner of Christ, must be, like His, a tough one. Especially, I repeat, when it comes to getting out of bed.

We may disagree on many different points but when it comes to the question of sleep, we are all as one. We all need it. In itself, sleep is a wonderful thing. It is the cure-all, the reliever of pain and weariness, the silent state that provides temporary escape from harsh reality. It offers security to the fearful, refuge to the needy, and balm to the man who is just plain "worn out." Because it is one of the few things in life that is free, anyone may have it. The principal requisite is a horizontal position, although some people can sleep in a chair. We even have a Brother who is so clever that he is able to fall asleep while standing. But such an attitude, being very temporary as well as precarious, cannot be safely recommended.

When night falls and the day has taken its heavy toll of the human body, a man pulls the covers up to his chin and goes to sleep. Few would ever think of depriving him of this; for when a man sleeps his conduct is above all reproach. He is as far removed from mischief and deceit as he could ever be.

Having established, therefore, the wide proposition that all men sleep, it may logically be deduced that friars sleep. Actually, with so many atheistic scoundrels running roughshod over the earth, the work of God would require a twenty-four hour working day. But who can do it? The saints, of course, approached this — but they were saints. Some of them must also have been magicians. Meditation books tell us that St. Peter Alcantara slept on a rope. Trying to visualize his extraordinary feat does not make for serious meditation. But whether we sleep on ropes or flagpoles, the length of monastic repose has been determined by qualified spiritual writers, who tell us that any more than six hours is sheer laziness. So we take six hours and we are sincerely grateful for every last one of them.

What happens in a monastery at break of day? How are the men aroused from their slumber? Is it gentle or is it violent? Is it fast or slow? Noisy or silent? For anyone who might ask himself these questions, let us put it this way.

When Brother Disturbus hears (in so many Latin words) at the reading of assignments on Saturday that he is bell ringer for the week, he knows that he is in for something. For one solid week, by virtue of his thankless duty, he must acknowledge himself as the lowest form of animal life. His is the serious obligation of leading the community from one exercise to another, and the fact that his bell is the voice of God offers him scant consolation. He must furnish oil for the smooth-running mechanism of monastic routine. He must constantly be synchronizing unpredictable timepieces. Finally (and this is the most bitter pill of all), he must awaken the community at the start of each day.

Ordinarily, Disturbus starts work at 4:30 A.M. He rises from his board with sad intent, works some life into his limbs, and hurriedly gets himself washed and dressed. By 4:40 he is standing at the end of the first long corridor, armed with a wooden "clapper" and hating himself for the thing he is about to do. But it must be done because God is waiting in the chapel. The world is waiting for the sacrifice.

The duties of Brother Disturbus in this specific phase are relatively simple. He first rattles the clapper causing it to resound with the volume of several machine guns until the clamor reverberates into every corner of every cell. Nothing escapes its terrible summons. No one can honestly say, "I didn't hear it." Then he begins the second part of the process. Raising his voice in a commanding fortissimo, he entones his morning song: *"Praised be Jesus Christ and His Virgin Mother. Arise, Brothers, to pray and praise the Lord."* Then he starts down the corridor, pausing to knock at each door, hard or soft according to the dictates of his temperament for that day. Only after hearing the thin response of *"Ave Maria"* from the poor soul inside, does he move on to the next door, recalling as he goes the words of the Psalmist, *"I will rise in the middle of the night to praise Thy Holy Name."*

But behind those closed doors another drama is being enacted, and it is a sad one. Brother Rock cautiously opens one eye and becomes conscious of his existence. But with this consciousness comes his first prayer which might have been included in the *Raccolta* except for one thing — it doesn't work. He prays, *"O Lord and Saviour Jesus Christ, who of old didst say unto Thy Apostles, 'Sleep on and take thy rest,' grant I beseech Thee, that I too may sleep on and take my rest."* But the voice of God comes down from heaven: *"There is no rest for you, Rock. Get up to pray and praise Me for the day is now far spent."* Rock slowly eases himself out of his bed. He has been told by his Superior that all religious should get up as if their bed were on fire. But fire is so warm; the cell is so cold. Feeling his way for the light, he switches it on, returns and sits again on the edge of his bed. He looks down at his sandals on the floor and wonders sleepily why one is pointing north and the other south. He puzzles over the miracle of electricity. He visually tracks the course of a crack that runs up and down his wall. Everything is so confused.

But time is flying, so he hustles through his ritual of a quick dress and even quicker wash, drags himself to the staircase, and in the company of his brothers, awaits the sound of Disturbus' five o'clock bell that will send him into the choir for a two hour stay. As he stands there he thinks, "The early bird gets the worm. But who likes worms anyway?"

Most of us, I suppose, are like Brother Rock. But once in a while an "odd job" springs up in our midst.

Such a one was Brother Gustave. He enjoyed getting up. On those many nights when we lined up in double file preparatory to going down for the midnight office, Brother Gustave would trundle his way through the line, smiling and waving at us as he passed. We who stood like warmed-over corpses could not stand this. Oh, how we hated him for his unique freedom from the agony of vacating the sack! Still, he turned out to be a fine priest.

The story of monastic sleep is a story of endless sacrifice. By our own free choice we rarely, if ever, know the joy of being able to "sleep ourselves out." Day after day, year after year, we still get up. And nothing will ever change it. It is difficult because the drawn-out burdens are hardest to bear. Burdens come better in lumps. But it keeps us from going soft; it gives us a share in the sufferings of life. Besides, we are doing it for God. That makes it much easier.

But oh, how we men look forward to the day when we can begin our eternal slumber. I know that someday they will roll me up the aisle of our church for the last time. The Prior will stand by my box with incense and holy water and he will chant the ancient prayer of the church, "Eternal rest grant unto him, O Lord . . ." Eternal rest — what a wonderful prospect!

⟫ III ⟪

Let Us Pray

THE screening process for the admission of candidates to the religious life must of necessity be a rather rigorous one. Besides being rational, one must have average intelligence, average health, suitable disposition, and a proper intention. For admission to a monastery, the applicant must also be a male.

Then when the superiors have determined that one is neither heretical nor married; when they have ascertained that no force or undue fear or violence has been brought to bear on the subject; when they have satisfied themselves that the young man in question does not enjoy a prison record; when these and other factors have been investigated, then they are ready to consider an application.

But thank God, nowhere, either in our Constitution or in Canon Law itself, can there be found any such statement as "Only those are to be admitted into the novitiate who have achieved high proficiency in prayer." In other words, admission into a contemplative order does not require that an applicant be a contemplative. Only that he desires to be one.

I think that it would be the height of presumption on the part of any one of us to say that we were true-blue contemplatives on the day we entered the monastery. None of us was a master in the art of prayer. Oh, we had done our share of praying. We had attended thousands of Masses, said thousands of rosaries, were faithful to our morning and night prayers — but contemplatives! Not really. In fact, we were way out in left field. Not that there was anything wrong with that, but the world we left just wasn't geared to the production of contemplatives. On the contrary, everything was action. Use your hands, run, jump, talk, sing. Do anything. Just get busy. Was it any wonder that we were to have no little difficulty in tapering ourselves off to lead a life that would make us not toilers in the field but workers on our knees?

Which meant that we had a lot to learn. And pity the poor Novice Master who had to teach us. He had to begin at the beginning. So the first morsel he gave us was a high pressure explanation of the need for contemplation in today's world. But he had to go and sandwich these thoughts between two shocking statements: (1) prayer is never easy, and (2) digging a hole for three hours is often more agreeable than doing one hour of mental prayer. This did not help us much. But, as I say, he had a tough job. He had to sit up there and make prayer appealing to a gang of kids with inexhaustible sources of adrenalin. He had to teach us how to use with profit the two solid hours that are given over each day to mental prayer in all Discalced Carmelite monasteries. And his job was all the more difficult because the very mention of the word "contemplation" was enough to give us ulcers. To our un-

trained minds it meant loneliness and isolation. It meant a life entirely bereft of even the smallest and most innocent comforts. If the phrase could have had a color, it would have been black. But we bent ourselves to the task. If this was really something good, if it was something that God wanted and the Church needed, then we were glad to have a share. We really didn't want an easy life or we would never have come here. We weren't looking for any short cuts so we lowered our heads to receive what we thought was to be a glorious crown of white martyrdom.

Surprisingly enough, learning about contemplation did not hurt. Even with all the juggling of nebulous terms like Active Quietude, Passive Recollection, and Transforming Union we soon were able to decide for ourselves that contemplation is prayer, and prayer is nothing more than a "conversation with God, who we know loves us."

The system we were taught to use was relatively simple. We learned that prayer, like an examination, takes preparation. So fifteen minutes before the hour of prayer, a clapper sounded to announce that now was the time to get ready for converse with God. The purpose was to put the brake to an active mind and to ferret out any imagery that would very easily lead to distractions.

With the beginning of prayer itself, the assigned reader of the week read a few lines from a meditation book. (Meditation books may make good reading; they don't always make good meditation.) With the reading finished, we put our imagination to work, gave color to our thoughts, gave them shape, size, and reality. Which ultimately brought us to the essence of all prayer — conversation with God. Call prayer whatever you will, call it mental or vocal, infused or acquired, the prayer that is really prayer is the time spent in an intimate chat with the Creator. From this point a soul begins its work; from this point a soul goes out to all degrees of contemplation. And this is possible for anyone.

Is it easy? Well, apparently not. Of course, there must be some who have no difficulty in prayer. They are the ones who cannot tear themselves away from chapel, who are restrained as by some divine magnetic force; and although we thank God for their presence among us, we still must admit that their housework usually suffers. But for the greater number of us, prayer is not always a spiritual picnic. But then we are at it not for the pleasure we get from it, but for the pleasure we give to God by our willing sacrifice. And we pray not because it is easy, but because it is hard. Whether we receive consolation or not is of little consequence. The important thing is that we are there. We are trying. We are reaching out for God, searching for this Illusive Stranger, plumbing the depths of our shallow mind in quest of Him. And we never know but that the next hour of mental prayer might bring with it an experience that is rarely given to men. And, of course, we might never receive anything like it. But if God someday decides to bless us with a special gift of prayer, we want to be there when it comes.

People are bound to ask, "You who are professedly contemplatives, how is it that you have difficulty in prayer? We in the world, we are expected to have trouble praying. But not you!"

It all boils down to one thing. If we are all human (and I think we are), then we are all subject to the same blights of human nature. That is why, being men, we meet in our prayer the triple retarder of weariness, dryness, and distraction. These things do not nullify the efficacy of prayer but they do make it increasingly tedious.

First of all, why must we succumb to weariness during prayer? Why must this cross slow down our reactions, numb us, smother us so that all our efforts are aimed at simply staying awake? Yet, sadly enough, this happens sometimes. But we keep trying. In our novitiate days Brother Bertram was always tired. Many times in the silence of the choir, with gentle warmth hissing from the radiator, amid the shadows and the dim lights, Bertram would ask: "Dear God, why must I always be so tired?" But he never got any answer. The day came when he thought that by making his prayer while standing, he would be able to keep himself alive and radiant, but he toppled over the brother in front of him. That has been known since as "Bertram's last stand."

Then there is dryness. You kneel there and look in vain for some light. You seek out a bit of God's warmth, yearn to drink at the fountains of living water like the hart, but there is nothing. So you pray and you pray and you pray.

And distractions! A novice expects so much from his life. He believes that in time he will arrive at a certain stage wherein he will be above such lowly things as distractions. But always they are there. We cannot seem to leave our preoccupations outside the door of the choir. We cannot check our thoughts as we could check our hat or coat. Despite our efforts we drag them into choir with us. Always the unwritten sermon, the unsolved case, the unfulfilled obligation, or the hapless sinner — worries big and small, coming with us to our prayer, stealing our thoughts away from God, making us hate ourselves for our innate weakness. Still we pray.

You see, it is all we have. We have seen the needs of the world. We have divined our own inability to cope with the monstrosity of sin in our midst. We have become aware of the restriction in having only two hands with which to nurse the cosmic illness of our day. So we have turned in prayer to God who can accomplish all good. *We* could only work in remote corners but God with His power and His mercy can reach out to the world. So we leave it up to God.

Does it work? Is it worth it? Well, if it isn't, if prayer does not work, if the contemplative life is a big hoax, then we have wasted our lives. And if we have wasted our lives, all I can say is that nobody has ever paid such a high price for failure.

Let the man who does not believe in prayer, forget prayer. We shall pray. And in the end we shall see who comes out on top. For no one can possibly give himself over to prayer without arriving at a greater knowledge of God. No one can possibly dedicate his life to contemplation without someday finding, even while on this earth, a portion of heaven, a share in the divinity, and a wisdom that can be surpassed only by our eventual participation in the Beatific Vision itself.

❧ IV ❧

Sweet Is the Yoke

IN THE early days of our novitiate year we were forced to walk with uncertain steps through the intricate pattern of our new surroundings. Everything surprised us. Everything amazed us. We laughed at the wrong times and in the wrong places — especially in chapel. Periodically, we cried. Not so much with our eyes but with our hearts because sometimes life seemed to be so hard, and at other times because we felt so small before the towering beauty of our vocation.

Guarding ourselves and our actions as carefully as we could, we still blundered into impossible situations; floundered there for a while until, gathering ourselves together, we blundered out of them again. Such as the time at midnight office when Brother Myles went down behind the pew to plug in the electric organ, and fell asleep on the floor. Things like that should never happen to anyone. Or when hungry Brother Ronald slipped into the kitchen, eased open the refrigerator door and saw a sign on the rare platter of cream puffs, "Brother Ronald — get out of the ice box. There are just enough for the community." This takes the starch out of a man. Or on Halloween night when Brother Titus, almost at the end of his rope for want of some diversity of action, unhitched the door of a classmate's cell, started on his way to hide the thing in the shower, and in the darkness clashed with the tall, dynamic, horrible figure of the Novice Master. These are things we can never forget. At the time they made some of us wish we were dead. Only the thought that others like ourselves had persevered through similar ordeals kept us forging ahead.

One phase of community life, however, that gave us no end of trouble was the recitation of the Divine Office in choir. The first time we opened a breviary, all we could see was a mad confusion of red and black letters boxed in by red and black lines. It was a thick book, with red edges, and possessed a strange faculty for adding weight to itself while being held at one o'clock in the morning. In this we found something far more complicated than our daily Missal. But with the passing of the days we listened attentively to the instruction of the Master, reviewed, prepared, rehearsed, until we were finally admitted to the participation of the active Office, the recitation of the breviary in common.

But this was murder. We might have been able to go through the whole Office as we sat on a chair in our cells. But now, like a cog in the wheel, we were expected not only to work along with the crowd, but to do our own little solo in some specified section of the choir. This made the difference.

For Office in choir is not something dead. It is very much alive. There is movement and change and progressive continuity. When everything clicks, it is a thing of beauty, of deep edification. The chant soars, rises to the heavens, drawing with it all the greatest hopes and aspirations of men.

But in the novitiate, things did not always click. Instead of orderly maneuvering there was gentle chaos, novices saying the wrong thing in the wrong place at the wrong time; a heart-rending swarm of lost boys doing skids and turns, making bows big and little, sliding here, sliding there — all in the middle of the choir. When someone would be nudged off to the side, he would stand there a while aghast at his singularity then plunge back into the anonymity of the crowd. Until it all became a milling fantasy of scared kids with scared faces, and with eyes that saw nothing but an ocean of red and black letters boxed in by red and black lines. All this, and the exasperated look on the face of Father Master as he stood heroically struggling for patience, and no doubt saying within himself, "O God, give me strength."

Time alone, time and bitter experience, brought knowledge of the art of recitation in choir. With that knowledge came the knack of proper action. And with all this, the smooth running glory that is the chant of the Divine Office.

True, even after the rubrics were mastered, there were still difficulties. There was the monotonous standing and sitting when we were utterly weary. There were the required profound bows of the body when we barely felt like dipping our heads. There was the ever present problem of keeping the tone up to a working level. And always the questions. Are there any commemorations? *What* are they? *Where* are they? What

page are we on? What day is it? Do I say this? The
questions were always there. There was the burden of
the summer heat when perspiration blinded our eyes,
and falling, made little wet spots on the text of the
second nocturn. There was the endlessness of it all.
Office today. Office tomorrow. Office forever.

Yes, this indeed was the work of God and of such
we had no doubts. But it was also the burden of the day.
This was the sacrifice, the pushing of self when we
yearned only for rest. This was the driving victory of
minds over the dragging sluggishness of bodies. This
was a gift to God that hurt. A cross that cut. But all
this is what made it worth while — and this is probably
why we loved it.

From the very beginning we were made aware of
the grave and serious obligation that would always be
ours to recite this Office. But we were made no less
aware of the privilege that was ours to stand in the
person of all men and chant the praises of God for
the good of the Church and the salvation of souls. We
received the right to harmonize with angels at the feet
of the Lord. We were blessed to sing the chants of the
suffering Christ; to raise our voices in joy at His victory.

Of all the men on the face of the earth, we were the
relative few who had been chosen to pray for those
who would not or could not pray. We had been given
the right to use the official prayers of the Church which
in the matter of sheer beauty and expressiveness stand
unsurpassed. We lived every mood of the prayers we
sang. Felt every pain. Experienced every joy. We wept
with those lamentations of the Old Law which foretold

the immolation of the Lamb. We rejoiced in the relentless poundings of the glorious *Alleluias*.

All this was, and is today, our privilege and our heritage as men of God. So we make our voices rise and fall in the unique cadences of the chant. We might be expected to kneel down and kiss the floor when we have made an obviously incorrect addition or omission. We might wish at times that the long chanting of prayers would come to an end, and all the constant movement cease. We might feel acutely our unworthiness to intercede with God for those who might have been, if given the opportunity, far better than we ourselves are. Still, we are the ones to do this. It is our life, our love, our sacrifice.

But easy or hard, it is always a consolation to know that in days when men have plotted to upset the throne of God on earth, when they have stood defiantly before their Creator with jutting jaws and hard, glowering eyes, it is a consolation for us to be able to stand in choir with our breviaries in our hands and make reparation for the sins of the world, to pray in its behalf.

And for each blasphemy that is spewed recklessly toward heaven, the friars in their brown and white can turn their eyes to the tabernacle, and with their many voices praying as one, keep the pages turning and the plea ever resounding, *"Spare us, O Lord, spare thy people. And be not angry with us forever."*

✺ V ✺

Tonsorial Homicide

THE first time that I ever sat back into the monastery barber chair, I almost lost my left ear lobe. It was nothing serious but it made me wary of our monk barbers, and rather dubious over the grim depths to which they might possibly slip. I would not say that the monastery barbershop was the scene of frequent bloodshed; but I would say that many sad things happened under those dim lights. To be literally snatched bald was not just a funny saying in there. Hair was removed in swathes — as was the meadow grass in Belloc's account of mowing a field in his book *Hills and the Sea.*

This situation was the fault of no one. After all, whether in or out of the monastery, a man's hair grows. It has to be cut. And because it was not every day that a professional barber joined our ranks, then of necessity, we had to train our own barbers. Added to this problem was the fact that men moved, with the years, from one house to another. This means that trained barbers left and new ones had to be broken in.

I myself was never chosen to cut hair in the monastery, but I always wanted to say this to those who were: "We really aren't particular about the results of twenty minutes in your chair. We willingly submit to the clippers in your fumbling hands because in religious life we cannot be worried about how our heads look. There are too many important things. We don't care how we look because nobody else cares how we look either. Such vanity must die. All we ask is that the job be somewhat decent so as not to distract our fellow brothers at prayers. Help us keep our self-respect."

Actually, the barber shop itself was in no way conducive to fancy hair cutting. There were no full-length, lighted mirrors on the wall. There were no mirrors at all. When the barber said, "You're finished and you look fine," you took it on faith alone. No long line of bottles of brightly colored hair shampoos filled the shelves. There were no shampoos. In fact, there were no shelves. There were no calendars on the wall. The only pieces of equipment were the chair, a hanging light, and a box containing clippers, scissors, combs, and a battered carton of "Oriental Powder" with the subtitle, "The Ancient Fragrance of the East." The chair was not given to tricks. It did not move backward or forward. It did not go up or down. Therefore when a tall barber cut the hair of a little friar, he ended up with a kink in his back. And when a little barber cut the hair of a tall friar, he finished with aching arms. It was all mixed up.

I knew of only one professional barber who ever joined the Order — Brother Felix. Along with his ability to make false teeth, he was licensed to practice his tonsorial artistry in three states. Brother Felix was always a good barber, ever willing to cut the hair of a visiting retreat master or of any other guest at the monastery. He

knew his job, but that is exactly what caused him such anxiety and worry. I can still hear Brother Felix sighing in harmony with the quick, adroit snipping of his scissors (and close on the eve of his profession): "Boy, oh, Boy! Out in the world now barbers are getting a dollar a head, and here I am working over bumpy, odd-shaped noggins for free." And he had a case there.

But whether a man was a professional like Brother Felix or strictly an amateur like Brother Jude (and the rest), our monk barbers were all the same in as far as they were doing a good job "for free" and without complaint. This was commendable in view of a situation that gave the community barber no extra consideration, nor any time strictly set aside for cutting hair. He worked in his free time. At any hour of the day he could be called upon to don his muslin frock, spread a piece of sheet over his patient, and work the shag out of a head. We usually deemed it a penance to give up twenty minutes of our seemingly precious time to the uncomfortable but necessary process of getting our ears lowered.

The monastery barber with his clippers and comb is just another spoke in the ever turning wheel of religious life. He is part of the team, a member of the family. He is there to serve those who need his services. And his attitude and constant labor for others is like a fresh breeze in a world where men are taken up completely with the occupation of "self." The Brother Barber with his battered carton of "Oriental Powder" is a silent challenge to the world. Through the practice of his art he stands to prove that life is wonderful even without the gratification of personal interests. And his is the contention that the greatest happiness of all is the happiness that comes from giving his time, his effort, and his work for the benefit of others. And "others" is the key word. He doesn't care what it costs him — just as long as it is for others. Added to this he knows that his office of cutting hair, though commonplace in itself, is still an important phase in the over-all plan of saving souls.

How well he knows what Sacred Scripture says, "The hairs of your head are numbered . . ." and the number runs into the millions. He knows hair as he knows heads, our barber does. He knows the smell of that ancient fragrance of the East. He knows the odor of an overheated clipper and the metallic click of speedy scissors. And whether he likes it or not is nobody's worry. Because whether he likes it or not, he will keep hacking away. He will never run out of work; neither will he ever run out of the will and the determination to do that work.

He might not be the best barber in the world. But if he does slip and take off part of somebody's ear, he will be right there to slap a band-aid over the wound, pat his victim on the head, and say, "You're doing fine. Hold your head straight and stop wiggling." And the soft, gentle snip of his shears will ascend as his rebuttal to the biblical admonition, "And him who will not work, neither let him eat."

≫VI≪

The Salve Regina Hour

FROM the very beginning little Brother Myles was a high-calibered product of the Discalced Carmelite way of life. With the thrill of his new existence still vibrant and warm within him, he worked hard to master perfection in the Order to which God had ever so deftly directed him. Comprehending with clear perception the spirit of prayer that was foremost in his chosen state, and understanding also the spirit of penance and solitude that he hoped would bring him in closer contact with his Creator, Brother Myles had, in a short time, come a long way in religious life. He was, in fact, way ahead of us all.

But nothing, not even the oldest habits of his brief religious life, had become so deeply embedded within him as the horarium, or order of the day. So, when the large brass bell would ring out at five minutes to eight every Saturday night, he knew just what was coming off. If he was reading, he closed his book. If he was writing, he put down his pen. Whatever was functioning within the restricted confines of his tiny cell, came abruptly to an end, and snapping off his light, he would step out into the deep shadows of the corridor and make his way toward the chapel. By that

35

time, the halls would be faintly alive with the scuffle
of sandaled feet, and into this marching regiment of
unglamourized monasticism, Myles would merge himself.
It would carry him along to the row of white mantles
hanging on hooks outside the sacristy door.

The crowd of us who gathered there was made up
of all types. There were the long, gangling friars of
sparerib proportions, the short fat ones, and the simple,
run-of-the-mill physiques — the whole line-up constitut-
ing a somewhat formidable wall of brown as Brother
Myles would work his way to hook number six, where
his own mantle hung. No one quite understood why
he had cut a big red number six from an old calendar
to paste above his hook, for there was no mistaking
Brother Myles's mantle. Its tiny size distinguished it
from all the rest. For he was the smallest friar in the
monastery, the smallest friar in the province. In fact, as
he so often put it himself (and sadly), he was probably
the smallest friar in the world.

But on Saturday night as he clothed himself in white,
he would realize that fellow Carmelites on every con-
tinent were doing the same thing. And he would wonder
how he had ever managed to get in on this Saturday
night treat to our Lady, this token of love for God's
mother and his own, the *Salve Regina*. While he stood
in line wearing the color that was symbolic of his
purity and holding a burning candle in his hand,
Myles would think about Mary who was the patroness
of his Order and the light of his life. He admitted to
himself that someday as a priest he would not be able
to save even one soul without the help of Mary; that

as a man, he would not even be able to save his own soul without her.

When eight o'clock struck, the community would file out into the sanctuary — first the lay brothers, then the clerics, the priests, two acolytes, a brother with the holy water and finally, the esteemed Father Prior in a flowing silk cope. Lined up on both sides of the sanctuary, running straight down from the foot of the altar to the communion rail, a small army of personified devotion, the friars would join their voices to the first peals of the organ, *Salve Regina, Mater Misericordiae,* "Hail Holy Queen, Mother of Mercy." Walled in by the rising heights of big Brother Berthold on his left and big Brother Hubert on his right, Brother Myles would be all but hidden from the eyes of men. But it did not faze him. He would simply thrust his candle a bit higher so that Mary would not overlook his presence and join with full heart into the solemn beauty of the chant. Myles did not know much about harmony or counterpoint, and his voice, like most of the others, was untrained in the finer points; but he would sing his best and make his chant what it should always be, a prayer.

"Hail Holy Queen," little Myles would pray, "all that I live for and hope in, my Sweetness. Here I stand crying up to you in self-chosen banishment from the things of the world. Here I pray with ascending sighs, conscious of sorrow and tears, and burdened with my dose of the taints of original sin. Look down upon me, Mary, now as I live; but when this exile is over, bring me to heaven where I may see in all His glory your divine Son. Mother of meekness, Mother of pure love, Mother of sweetness, pray for me and for all these men here who are far better than I and perhaps more loved by you. Pray that they may become great saints and I, a little saint. For being the smallest friar in the world, I was made for little things, but whatever you make us, see to it that we are someday worthy of redemption."

At the final notes of the chant, Father Prior, receiving the aspergill, would start around the sanctuary to flick tiny blobs of holy water upon the heads of his subjects. Brother Myles, leaning out from between his towering companions, would catch a drop and bless himself, then go into a deep bow with the rest of the community for a silent "Our Father." And while he prayed he could not help seeing the smallest pair of sandals in the world and an ingrown toenail that was forever making him realize the inescapable factor of little pains in life, that perfect relief would only come in heaven.

Then when the *Salve* was at an end, the brothers would come to the center of the altar, genuflect two by two, and as they started into the sacristy, the low monotone of the *De Profundis* would rise to their lips. Brother Myles would say this prayer with all the reverent enthusiasm he could muster. After all, this psalm meant liberation or relief for the souls who languished in Purgatory. So he would say it for them just as he would want others to say it for him when he had hung his mantle on hook number six for the last time.

It was his gracious gift to all those men who had sung

the *Salve Regina* on Saturday night for centuries back, Discalced Carmelites like himself. Time had borne them into another world and they had left a vacant place in the white line-up. Some day Brother Myles would also leave a vacant place and nothing could ever change it. But as he passed through the door on Saturday nights, the Mother whom he had honored, probably felt that it would take a very big man indeed to fill up the little opening that Myles would leave when he went to collect his great reward.

⇛ VII ⇚

Quiet, Please

Any young man with an insatiable passion for speech will hardly make a success of life in a monastery. He will discover that religious life has surrounded the wonderful gift of speech with many positive snaffles; that words and the expression of ideas have been relegated to periods of recreation.

One rarely enters a monastery bearing with him the infused gift of silence: it, as all other monastery habits, must be acquired. All of us had to learn how and when to keep our mouths shut. But, with silence all over the house, prevailing like the wind, we had no reason for not being able to fall in step with the life around us. Training in silence was the order of the day, every day, through the months of novitiate. We were happy to have an opportunity to speak to one another each day at recreation periods, but we were also satisfied to keep the silence when we were supposed to because of the good that was bound to come of it.

And although it would hardly seem possible, when Lent came that first year, there was an even greater than ordinary silence pervading the halls of Carmel. Or seemed to be. The clicking of rosary beads was softened. Disturbing squeaks were routed from sandals.

Voices were hushed. Even the telephone did not ring as stridently as usual, or the doorbell. And the cook did not seem to bang the pots and pans as loudly as was his wont. Life within the monastery had become a giant in soft shoes, aggravating its own silence, not because of any special regulations, but only because Lent at the novitiate seemed to spawn an even greater and more profound silence. That year, for the first time in our lives, we let the cloak of quiet fall about our shoulders completely. For the first time we were able to think even deeper thoughts about the Man who went by with a cross. Silence can do that.

But the virtues of this quiet are all so incomprehensible to many people. I do not think that we are far wrong in saying that, on the whole, men are not too appreciative of the virtue of silence. Living today is a chaotic struggle at high speed. The faster people go, the more noise they make; and the more noise they make, the better they feel. For they are afraid of silence. Silence makes them think, and they do not want to think, because when they do, their thought processes gradually sweep them before the unwavering eyes of a just God. They do not like that at all. It hurts; it frightens. So they run and they shout — always pretending. Like little boys they whistle themselves past a cemetery pretending it is not there.

The antithesis of silence is noise, and the greatest single enemy of silence is conversation — talk. Some people talk as naturally as champagne bubbles. We have it from a reliable authority that average Americans use about 30,000 words in the passing of an ordinary day — the equivalent of a fair-sized book. We impose, force, spew all these words upon our friends, enemies, and associates in general. It means that if these people had not listened to us, they might have read a good book that would have been of genuine benefit to their souls. How worth while were our 30,000 words? Actually, most of our conversation has no more merit or effect than to stir the air around us. Consequently, we could all say so very much less without any fear of the world's becoming worse. In fact, if we practice with greater fidelity the virtue of the closed mouth, the world would probably be the better for it.

Not only that, but God alone knows all the grief we have caused ourselves by the imprudence and over-indulgence of our tongues. Many were the times when we felt like kicking ourselves halfway around the block for having said something we shouldn't have said. And sometimes we felt as if we would have given our right arms to have some of our spoken words revoked. No doubt about it, silence is good sense for everybody. Too bad we can't love it more!

"Silence braces the sinews of the soul"; it reinforces the powers of the mind. This is why it is so widely practiced in all religious communities. But, of course, it is not always easy. There are times when, catering to the gregariousness of our natures, we like to gather in groups and solve the problems of the day with our wise verbosity. Certainly when we entered religious life like hot cakes off the sizzling griddle of the world, we didn't get this business of silence. Like many other things, it went over our heads in the beginning. All it required was a little time for us to realize the wisdom of the closed mouth. We finally took St. James at his word when he said, "If any man sin not with his tongue, the same is a perfect man."

After years of seasoning we would come to see the reason for it all. We would find that through silence we could begin to live in a world that would not be laid open to the penetrating wheeze of high pitched voices or the gruff cursings of the basso profundos. We would come to appreciate silence for the splendid opportunity it would give us to see all things in their true light. We would always be grateful for the lesson it would teach us — that the less we say, the more effect and weight our words will carry when we do speak. And we would come to accept silence not as a form of capital punishment (as some would) but as a reprieve from the overpowering pressure of ordinary living. In silence we would find rest, not boredom. And what is more, we would actually come to enjoy it.

The Prophet Elias found God where he least expected Him. Elias was a complete extrovert, a rugged, brawling servant of the Lord. He used a harsh, violent display of power to overcome his enemies. Zeal poured from him as he thundered across the plains of Palestine. But he looked for God in the wrong places, tried to find Him in his own personal type of element, in the storm, the earthquake, the fire. And he never found God until he slowed himself down and looked elsewhere. Finally, it was the soft, gentle breeze that brought God to him. In the silence of the desert, he found God. Probably that is where all men must find

Him. At least, that is where men in monasteries try to find Him.

But then, we are religious. We are different. So we cannot expect the world to accept silence and treasure it as we have done. We cannot expect traffic cops to throw away their whistles or bus drivers to disconnect their horns. We cannot expect merchants to haggle in low, subdued voices; or cab drivers to transport their fares beneath a cloud of deep, sepulchral quiet. We

cannot expect any of these things. We *do not* expect them. We cannot hope that silence will subdue noise. We do not believe it is possible. But we do believe that if people said less, made less noise, they would be wiser. And with that wisdom would come the ability to cope more adequately with the complexities of living.

Noise and talk have not made us less human, but they have made us less wise. Because of it, we have sometimes crippled the growth of our culture and impeded the development of our knowledge. And the fact that some Americans have failed to adjust their mighty voices to their little worlds has turned them into some of the greatest bores on the face of the earth.

None of us should be too proud or too ashamed to admit that we have spoken too much and too often for our own good. And if some friend loves us enough to say, "shut your mouth," we should not condemn him for his insolence, but thank him for his advice. It is only too bad that God did not furnish zippers with every mouth He made. For if He had, we might more easily become intellectual giants. We might more easily become saints.

So when the five o'clock bell rings on these dark winter evenings, we go into our grand silence. We do this in an effort to achieve through external silence, the great prize, internal silence. For it is the internal silence that counts; it is the internal silence that gives us the power to remain ever unruffled, ever calm, ever the master of our surroundings. And blessed is he who can remain unruffled before the wild antics of modern civilization.

≫ VIII ≪

Bells

COMES the day toward the end of the novitiate year when you wake up in the morning with the conviction that since things can't get any worse, they are bound to get better. This is a good sign. It means that you have reached the top of the hill, the point of no return; and from here on in, it is all downhill. Almost. It is the moment of great transition when the things that seemed hard before, are not quite so hard any more. Crosses are not as heavy; pet peeves are fewer. Not that the life changes, only the mentality. You have at last become used to the life.

This, of course, is no phenomenon. Human beings can get used to anything. It is just the old story of a man adapting himself to his surroundings. I remember once when I was a little boy back in Germantown, something went wrong with our plumbing and the pressure went out of our water. All of a sudden, things became very inconvenient around the house. But after a few weeks of it, we adjusted ourselves to the nuisance and made it a part of our lives. We stopped fretting over the ageless wait for the bathtub to fill. We just started the trickle of water into the tub, went to the movies, and when we returned, the bath was ready.

Eventually, when the difficulty was adjusted, we didn't know what to do with all the water.

So in religious life, we adjusted ourselves to the presence or the lack of all things. We got used to the odd hours, the food, the hard beds. Therefore, we do not deserve either the sympathy or the admiration of those who look at us and say, "How do they do it?" Believe me, it is relatively easy.

More than any objects of sympathy or admiration, we should be the center of envy. Our whole existence has been simplified by the presence of a lowly little bell which contains within its inanimate self the power and the jurisdiction to stir a whole community into action. It is a bell that solves our problems, makes our decisions, gives us direction. It has freed us from much doubt. We need not worry about what is coming next, or when. At the sound of the bell, we move. We eat by it, sleep by it, walk and run by it. Nor do we have only one bell.

Any monastery is a jungle of bells. Outside of the obvious presence of bells on our front door and our telephones, there are bells for calling the brothers to class, there are bells for announcing the correction of faults, bells for paging the Fathers, bells for serving Mass. Every time one of them rings in a monastery, something happens. If nothing happens, it should. But of all bells, the greatest are those that hang high up in the tower of the monastery church. Nothing but time will remove them.

They rest silently there through heat and cold, until they are jerked into life by the hard hands of Brother

Finian, the sacristan. But when they do sound forth, they speak as no man can speak. They sing with the purity of the air and mold their voices to the phantoms of the shifting winds. Of all the bells in Carmel, these are the queens. For when they roll to lick their tongues against the hard metal of their sides, they have a message not for the few, but for all.

They awaken the countryside each morning, and the farmer sets his watch to their voice. They summon men to adore their God within the church. They are the messengers who hurl the word of His coming upon the altar of sacrifice. And through the day, the duty of announcing the Angelus is theirs. When they fulfill it, all human life within their echo doffs hats to praise our Lady.

They are the grand accompaniment to the joyous song of the *Te Deum*, rolling themselves to and fro in salute to him who dedicates his life by vow to God; or in tribute to any time of triumph throughout the year.

When a man has fallen asleep in the Lord, leaving the earth on which he labored to seek out in unknown horizons the reward of his life, the bells are there to weep and moan for him, to shed their tears of sound, to mark in slow and mournful cadence the scuffing of monastic sandals toward a monastic grave.

They are, too, the timepieces of brothers working on the far reaches of the property. They are the voice of God crying, "Come, Brothers, for your work is over. Come to your rest." And as they ring, men in brown drop their shovels and saws, cut the ignition of their trucks, lay down their paint brushes and slide rules and come together for the fulfillment of the common life.

These are the bells synchronized with every movement and pulsing of our life. Yet, it seems, they have become as the air around us — something taken for granted, discovered best when they cease to carry out their mission. We hear them and acknowledge them but rarely give a thought to the bells themselves. It is only when their ropes have been pulled too hard and they go tumbling into uselessness upon their backs that we must tend them and help in their restoration. Then we climb, most cautiously, the long, high web of a ladder that reaches up to their nest and turn them back with much exertion to their level of utility. And, descending, we admit to ourselves that they are not just things, but voices which possess within themselves the ability to re-echo the gamut of men's emotions, to whip out a cry of happiness or to rumble a hard, dark melody of grief. It is then that we realize we need them, for things could not be the same, nor would life go on in peacefulness without their guiding voices.

All these bells around us, they are lifeless; but they rule us who have life. Within the monastery, they are the voice of God. They are His messengers. Sometimes we find it comforting to hear them; sometimes not, but they keep order. They move us and keep us together. Since our salvation rests with helping one another in the common life, and since the bells provide such opportunities by keeping us together; then they are indeed (as they say) worth their salt.

Bells run things in our monastery, they run things in all monasteries; and with little doubt, they are here to stay.

❧ IX ❧

The Great Day

YOU answer the bells, take orders, work, study, pray. You try to convince yourself that everything has its greater compensations. You endeavor to be the very best novice that you can. Then, one day, it is all over. You have proved yourself.

It is wise of the Church to establish the canonical novitiate at only one year, because after twelve months and one day of it you've had enough. You're anxious to get on with it.

Therefore, with novitiate at an end, we were permitted to pronounce our vows. This was indeed a great day in our lives. On that beautiful August morning, with the altar banked with flowers, with the ringing of the bells and the solemn chanting of the *Te Deum,* our white cloaked brothers came together and watched us make the fullest possible dedication of our lives to God and the Blessed Mother by taking upon ourselves the vows of poverty, chastity, and obedience. They knew even better than we that our life would not be an easy one, that there was a softer way to save our souls. But like them, we chose the hard way because we believed with all our hearts that what we were doing was the best thing for us.

At the very beginning of the ceremony the superior put before us the simple question, "What do you seek?" In other words, we were given freedom to choose. It was as if we were asked, "What do you want most in the world? What is your heart's desire? You are young and strong, your potentialities of service to mankind are just short of infinite. So what can we give you?" But the response we gave was the only one we wanted to give. It was everything we wanted and the only thing we needed. "We ask for three things: The mercy of God, the poverty of the Order, the companionship of our brothers." It was so little, so very little, to ask of life. It seemed so paltry, so impossible. Yet, it was everything. With these three things crowding in on our lives, there would be no room for anything else. Nothing to clutter our pathway to God, neither barricade nor detour.

The mercy of God. It would come to us in profusion. It would overwhelm us. Like all creatures, we would stand before God someday for judgment. Then we would be faced with the record of our life. We would not like what we saw there. Smudges where there should have been clear prints, failures where there should have been successes, an inexcusable fall or an intolerable lapse. We would see ourselves as the type of religious we could have been, should have been in fact, but never were. Nor would we be able to blame human nature for our apparent spiritual bankruptcy. All that will be left for us to do will be to fall on our knees and pray, "Dear Lord, have mercy on us." And He probably will.

We asked for the poverty of the Order and the Order would see that we got it. After all, it is no trick to give away nothingness. Never again would we be able to say of any worldly thing, "This is mine"; for we had deprived ourselves of such a claim. We had denied ourselves the God-given right of private ownership. We would have nothing in the Order; yet we would share in everything that was contained in the Order. Furthermore, in asking for poverty, we were cast into the cauldron of common property wherein everything we might wear and use could be legally worn or used by anybody else.

Finally, we begged for the companionship of the brothers. Cognizant of the saint who said that community life was his greatest cross, we asked for this companionship with a sort of dubious enthusiasm. But there was no reason for doubt, as the passing of the years would prove. Seven of us made our vows; and seven of us would be ordained priests years later. With all due respect to vocation and the will of God and without any attempt to discredit the writings of saints, we probably turned in a perfect record because we were all in it *together*. No matter how tough things would get through the touchy years of studies, there would always be the helping hand and the consoling word from one of the gang. In seeking the companionship of our fellow religious we were to learn the meaning of real, genuine manly love. We would give it and receive it as a most prized possession. It would be able to soar above all barricades of race, color, mentality, or personality. We would give and receive freely of this friendship because we knew that nothing like it could be found anywhere else in the world. We would have acquaintances outside; but our friends were here. God picked them. So it would be God's work to keep our friendship ever shining through the veil of personal faults, of oddities and idiosyncrasies.

These were the three requests we made on the day of our profession. And when the superior was convinced that we were serious about it, he permitted us to advance one by one, to kneel at his feet and make our vows. When it was over, we stretched ourselves face down on the floor and while we were occupied with the problem of how to keep ourselves from smothering, he scattered bits of flowers upon us. Symbolic of death, supposedly, but far more symbolic of the freshness that would always seem to be somehow present in every day of religious life. Then we rose, faces reddened from their incarceration beneath heavy cowls, and went from one member of the community to the other, dispensing and receiving the kiss of peace. This marked the end of the ceremony. So we dropped into our places in line, different men by far from what we were one hour before.

From that day on we became in all reality a part of the Order we loved. We became sharers in the priceless heritage that had been preserved and passed down by souls who were great not because they were saints taken from among men, but because they were men who made themselves saints. We became a part of the great contemplative apostolate by joining ourselves to St. Teresa, "Mother of the Spiritual Life." We became integrated with an Order rich in missionary history, boasting its fair share of martyrs who shed their blood for God in foreign lands.

Of all these things we would become increasingly aware with each passing day. They would help us grow up in God. True, they might set us aside sometimes as a contradiction to the nations, but they would enable us to give purpose to and a reason for existence. And maybe because of what we were and what we became on our profession day, the world would raise itself a little higher from its squalor. This, at least, was our hope.

There is much that could be said about a profession but at the time we didn't know the whole story. But we would learn. We would come to know the world for what it was and still love it because it was so much in need of what God, through us, might give it. We would discover the difficulties of it all. Yet, we would always have the courage and the grace to lead men to God someday, simply because we found within ourselves the grace and the courage to kneel at the feet of our superior on profession day and say, "I promise poverty, chastity, and obedience, and all I ask in return is the mercy of God, the poverty of the Order, and the companionship of our brothers in Christ."

Student Days

The Hill

ONE beautiful morning with novitiate an accomplished fact, we prepared to head west for the house of studies. And we were happy about it. Not that we did not like the novitiate but, secretly, we were thrilled at the prospect of the trip. Between the novitiate and the house of studies there was a big world, filled with people (which we had so rarely seen for a year), overflowing with lights (other than the dim little things in our cells and our choir), and streaked with high activity (something that was still not killed within us). We looked forward to the trip because we thought it would work a few spiritual kinks out of our souls by bringing us to see and rub shoulders with the people to whose salvation we had dedicated our lives. Perhaps, in the intensive work of self-perfection we had forgotten that there is no such thing as a selfish pursuit of holiness, that we could never say, "I'm going to save my own soul and let the rest of the world go jump in the lake." (This is an attitude of which any contemplative must beware.) The trip would force us to cross the paths of many people who needed God and who needed our prayers. It would be a fine reminder.

So we lined up to say good-by to the Master. And I

still hate myself for what happened then. I moved forward to say good-by and literally stepped on his toes. And I thought in disgust, "What a mess, all year he nurses me through the spiritual life and now I have to go and smash his foot on the day I leave." He jumped a little, shook his head dolefully, smiled in a way that easily conveyed his thoughts, "Thank God, I'm getting rid of you." And just like that, we were off and running.

One thing about our house of studies, a friar just doesn't walk into it. He approaches it with reverence and this is no problem because the place is visible from ten miles out. With the old red truck humping wildly along the highway, with our trunks shaking precariously under us, we looked in wonder at its beauty. There it was. Holy Hill. The only place of its kind in the world, great and red and magnificent even from miles away. Greater yet, as we swung into Carmel road and up to the front door of the monastery.

We considered it no small privilege to hang our hats there. For this place was indeed Mary's. Thousands of Americans have never heard of it, let alone climbed it; but it has drawn countless numbers of Mary's friends from all over the country. Every year pilgrims come on trains and buses, cars, trucks, bicycles; they even walk —but they come. Thirty miles west of Milwaukee, off U. S. Highway 41, Holy Hill throws itself high into the Wisconsin skies. In fact, the crosses on the tops of the towers are just about as close to heaven as anything else in the entire state. The Air Force has stamped its location upon navigation maps as a guide for its pilots.

The Chamber of Commerce has listed it upon its tourists guides as a "must" for travelers. It has been for years a mecca of artists and photographers. Writers have lauded it with scratching pens and rattling typewriters Families have made it the goal of their Sunday rides in the country.

It was good to be a part of all this. It was good to be able to kneel down and pray not only for these people but with them. But things were not always like this. Fifty years ago the first Carmelites climbed the Hill. What they found there, and then what they made of it would be a great story. But it would have to be written in the hard language of hunger, cold, and poverty. It could not be told without such words as, "disappointments, setbacks, fear, and shattered hopes." But it grew. Every yard of lumber, every brick and bag of cement that went into the construction of the magnificent church on the top of the Hill was shipped from distant cities, loaded upon grinding old trucks that climbed until they could climb no more, then transferred to a cable elevator that crawled its way up into the sky. Yet, the job was done. A gem in brick and mortar, visible for miles around, a truly holy spot in a very godless world.

During our first winter there (and every winter thereafter) we knew what it felt like to be cut off from everything. The world left us alone. But with the coming of spring we saw things that we could never forget. Pilgrims came to pay homage to the Mother of God, the Lady Help of Christians. Young and old, they labored with their priests up the steep, winding way of the cross, sometimes with their feet bared to the cutting stones; climbed the hundreds of steps on their knees, atoning for their own sins, but more often for the sins of the world. Then on the summit they moved into the church and made their way to the shrine. There in the midst of a burning furnace of vigil lights they knelt to pray. No, we could never forget this. This and everything like it would convince us that the crazy old world wasn't so bad after all.

And then when the crowds were gone, we would go to make our own private pilgrimage to the shrine. We would kneel before that statue that was fashioned in Germany, displayed for a time at the Philadelphia World's Fair, then carried by eighteen young girls over the seven hard miles from the nearest railroad depot. We would look with wonder at the crutches and braces, these badges of helplessness stacked up against the side walls of the chapel, and visualize those who left them there to walk away, sound of limb, with singing hearts and with their eyes blinded by tears. But all the while we would know that the crutches told only half the story, failed to bear witness to all the miracles of mind and soul that Mary has worked in our own country and for our own people. And with all this we knew that our lives could never be the same again.

Small wonder then that we were so happy to be a part of all this. Even in the medieval atmosphere of our refectory, the food seemed better tasting. And the view from our cells is worth a million dollars. We were able to stand there and let our vision shoot straight out for thirty miles and maybe scan from left to right double that. We were able to see the smoke of trains but never hear them; to watch men, untouched by the high speed of a new civilization, tilling their fields by day. We drank water that was as cool and as fresh as the air; we watched birds and tiny beasts scurry through every tree. For up here man and nature mingled without conflict; sky and woods were common property.

The hard days of novitiate were over. Now we had all this. We were students all ready to tackle the books, enthusiastic over our new home. So we all shared a common belief, "We're students now. Life is going to be great. Yes, sir, great!" But oh how young and innocent we were. And how blind.

※XI※

Raw Material

THE sun kept shining; the wind kept blowing. We couldn't change that; in fact, we couldn't change anything. We were only students. Like all creatures of the same ilk, something went wrong within the empty cavern of our minds. We thought that our vows had made something of us, and this is where we made our mistake. As far as the Order was concerned, we were still nothing. We were still down in some kind of a hole and it was entirely up to us to get ourselves out of it. We were only students.

Certainly it is a lot easier to write about a student than it is to be one. But if a man doesn't go through it himself, he cannot write about it. He wouldn't dare. For students are like candy canes, never true until they are twisted. So like all students, we were twisted. And although it never did us any harm, it was never easy to take.

First of all, we had to get an education. Not that an education is necessary for salvation, not that an education is necessary to make a man out of a child; but in our specific case, we had to learn something. It is true that men and women have become saints even though they *did* graduate out the window of sixth grade. But for our purposes, we had to face up to some very tough studies.

As long as the priesthood would be in question, it would be impossible to conceive of any man taking upon himself such a highly responsible dignity without acquiring a good, first-rate education. We wanted to be Carmelite priests. O.K., then we first had to be Carmelite students. There was no short cut, no flitting around the books, nothing but hitting them head on and licking them.

Being priests now, we know what it is to be a student. We've had it. So if at times, bent almost double beneath the yoke of our responsibilities, we sigh, "Oh, to be a student again," do not believe us. We are dreamers. It would be far more honest of us to admit that we feel sorry for our boys as we watch them lugging their ponderous philosophy books into the classrooms. And secretly, if we are willing to admit it, every time we see them, we are glad studying is behind us. We will never be in that spot again.

But we had to run the gauntlet. Many were the nights when we sat bleary eyed in our cells trying to memorize (for nothing else is possible) a Hebrew assignment for the next day. Or Greek. Or Latin. We never had enough time for it all. Then there were the dark days when we slunk into the chapel at votation time to sweat out a possible black ball for having faltered a little on the way. And more often than we like to think about, we blinked through our dry tears at the distant goal of priesthood and wondered if, through all the grind and the worry, we would ever reach it.

Nobody seemed to care about us. Or so we thought. We imagined that we stood all alone grappling with our common enemies — doubt and borderline despondency. But the superiors were watching. They saw us pass our changeless days, saddened perhaps at the things that saddened us, and pleased at the things that pleased us. They heard us in our classrooms stuttering to expound, with our yet untrained minds, the thought and history of centuries. They heard us in our recreation room, laughing at ourselves and at one another (because in religious life, with all its complex rituals, it is relatively easy to make a fool of oneself). And they saw us kneeling in the darkened choir at prayer time, and undoubtedly felt our bewilderment at the illusive, intangible beauty of this thing called contemplation. They saw all this. They knew it. But on many occasions they could not help us. Our struggle had to be for the most part a solitary one, waged in the solitude of our individual souls. Most of the time it is the only way to learn.

How we must have inadvertently galled our superiors by our inadequacies. How we must have ruffled the raw edge of their patience by our missteps and misquotes. But then, could our stupidity not be attributed to our inexperience?

After all, we still labored beneath a handicap. We still had not established that perfect conformity of self with monasticism. As we worked at the composite business of religious life, it had to be clear to them that we were still new — and even after a year, still foreign. We had not changed ourselves yet. There was the student with magic in his viens who had forever to stifle the yen to snatch a rabbit from the Prior's ample pockets. There was the one who was forced to practically sit on his feet every time he caught the rare sound of popular music. And there was the boy who loved the lights of the city but never saw them any more. Beyond these, there were others who still thought much about the boat they'd never sail any more, or the motorcycle they'd never straddle again, or the horse they'd ride no more across the far expanse of a farm. And the brother who as he sat on his straight backed chair thought of his lifeguard's throne on an American beach. It was not easy to shake off the old loves. All we could do was try. All we could do was to bend all our efforts in forgetting the past so that we might ultimately assume a new identity, one that would make us all the same, with a common burden in a common life, sharing the common hope of someday standing in a sanctuary and praying, "I will go unto the altar of God."

So what were we? Nothing really. Just a pile of raw material at the end of the line. A gang of kids who were just a little too cocksure, a little too proud. So we had to take the treatment as it was dished out to us. Before we could hope to be of any good to anybody we had to undergo a great change, emotionally as well as intellectually and spiritually. But until that happened we would still have to look on helplessly as our superiors shook their heads saying, "These are impossible. These will never do." All we could do was hang on to our ideals. And hope.

In our own minds there was no group of young men anywhere who were as conscious of their calling as we. None were as intent upon the future as we. We were sure of what we wanted. We saw glimmering in every cloud, be it pink or black, the chalice and the stole. We had a true bearing. And if we could not walk, we would crawl. We would even grovel upon the road until the day when we would be able to throw ourselves down before the outstretched hands of Christ to receive upon our heads the anointing oils of priesthood. That was where we were going. And we knew it.

We wondered if such a day would ever come. But it would. Like all those before us, we would get through it and we would find ourselves without the slightest regret over the hard things with which we had to cope during the years of training. Like all those before us, we would find our student days small payment indeed for the deathless satisfaction of becoming a priest. For such a life there is no substitute.

❊ XII ❊

Our Scanty Thanks

IT TOOK a few months for us to adapt ourselves to life within the house of studies which, although much the same as novitiate, did have something new to offer. Now we had to learn to live with the sort of genius who affixed philosophical theses to the bathroom mirrors in order to study while shaving. We had to learn how to look interested while older students hotly debated over obscure terms like "essence" and "existence." These, and the problem of acquiring the hauteur and poise of an intellectual giant, for the purpose of impressing our professors, so occupied us that by the time Thanksgiving came around we had decided that rather than being a place of mental anguish, the house of studies was going to be, with God's help, decidedly easy to take. Having found ourselves at last, we were able to enter into the holiday with a proper and well-balanced frame of mind.

At that time fat butchers had been pushing equally fat turkeys across meat counters in stores all over the country. Then the bird, well basted and brown, was set in the midst of plenty at the family tables while everyone gathered around to the merry tune of clinking glasses and unabated chatter.

Things in the monastery were a bit different. There

was no turkey on our table but there was cranberry sauce stacked up beside a better than ordinary fish. All the trimmings were there along with a mysterious salad that seemed better suited for exhibition than for consumption. There was ice cream for dessert. And, like the rest of Americans, we were thankful for the food before us.

But our thanks went deeper, as they naturally should. We were grateful above all else for just being where we were, serving God in a monastery; for that was our greatest happiness — our only happiness. To have been thankful for any sort of worldly goods would have been oddly presumptuous since we had nothing. To have been thankful for a type of work that merited a stout pay envelope would have been strangely contradictory, for we received no pay. And to have been thankful for comfort would have made even God laugh. And furthermore, to have bowed our heads in thanksgiving to the Almighty for having made us such wonderful, such sterling, such gifted characters would have been plain idiocy since the very purpose of our lives had made us the lowest of men and the outcasts of a worldly wise citizenry.

What were we to thank God for? I suppose that was each man's personal business. What went on in the next fellow's heart was impossible to determine.

Take old Brother Clausurus, for instance. He was the monastery porter. His life was doorbells; his apostolate, salesmen. He had to receive all comers with the corners of his mouth turned upward in spite of how he felt. As far as he was concerned, this was his way of saving souls. And it was never easy. He had to cover at all times the front door, back door, and side door, plus the telephone; and when everything rang at the same time, poor old Brother Clausurus went into a tight circle. What was the use? He was always on call, no time for rest or relaxation, ever tensed for the sound of some bell. That was his life. In the matter of worldly gain, what had he to be thankful for? Nothing.

Brother Sartor spent the working hours of his life hunched over a needle and thread. He lived among heavy bolts of brown wool. He was rarely without a spool of cotton or some kind of pattern nestled in his lap. The measuring tape lying over his shoulder seemed to be as much a part of him as his head. When he entered the Order, he knew absolutely nothing about a "back stitch" or a "corded seam" or the process known as "sewing on the bias." But he took the job, learned as he went, did it every day, always smiling, sewing, mending. In a material way, what had he to be thankful for? Not a thing.

Brother Coquus cooked, cleaned pots, cooked again and cleaned more pots. He spent the whole day, seven of them every week, working in the kitchen. And for the most part, nobody seemed to realize he was out there. Granted that he was the best cook in the world, what could a man do with fish and eggs that might look and taste different from one day to the next? If there was any man in this world who had a reason for throwing up his hands in disgust over the callused unconcern of his patrons, it was Brother Coquus. But the kettles still boiled and the garbage went out on schedule.

Had the world been good to him? Hardly.

But I suppose nobody thought of the things he did *not* have on that Thanksgiving Day. We were all there at the table, our napkins tucked in at our neck, thankful like all Americans for the bounty of God that gave us a government in which we were free to live out our lives in a monastery. Along with the pleasure of one another's company, our joy on that occasion sprang from the possession of God-given gifts. For our vocation. For the undying loyalty of our fellow Carmelites. For the sacramental presence of Christ in our hearts each morning. And for the golden opportunities to pray, to think, and to merit the heavenly rewards that we hoped were coming to us someday. This was our gratitude.

It was all this that made us happy through the days. It was this happiness that made us disregard all the little inconveniences, such as the habit that scratched and chafed in the heat of summer and yet was never quite warm enough in the cold of winter. And it was this very same happiness that found us lying in bed at night, the day at an end just as yesterday had ended and just as tomorrow would end, with rosary in hand and the silent, sincere prayer on our lips, "Thanks be to You, O Lord, for having put into our lives such tremendous, incalculable riches."

❧ XIII ❧

No Money

PRIEST, student, brother are all specific forms of the true generic "religious." Regardless of where we stood in the community, or of what we were or did, we were still religious. Even the right of a priest to say Mass made him no more a religious than the brother who served him. And that which made us essentially religious was the fact that we all had vows.

So we spent much time working for a fuller and more complete understanding and appreciation of our vows. We thought about them; we read about them. Every year a retreat master came in to tell us how miserable we were, and how much happier we would be if we lived our vows right to the hilt. And that was true.

In the early days of profession we felt very heroic at the thought of what we did. Because, at the time, we considered vows something like a ball and chain around our necks, we were amazed at the generosity that prompted us to give so much to God. It wasn't until later that we caught on and began to see that in making vows to God, we weren't giving up anything. We were receiving.

When I took the vow of poverty, I said to myself sadly, "Now I must be forever poor. Now I can never own anything again." Actually, I was no less broke after I took the vow than I had been before, so I don't know why I felt sorry for myself. Usually those who have the vow of poverty rarely feel the pinch of poverty.

People in the world do not have a vow of poverty; therefore, they have every right to own money. The only problem is how to get it. So money occupies people's minds almost constantly. That is why we hear statements like, "it doesn't matter if you're rich or poor, just as long as you have plenty of money" or what one working girl says to the other, "I've been poor and I've been rich, and believe me, honey, rich is better." So whenever we men find ourselves in some crowded neck of the world, such as the Chicago Loop, we can take it all in and say with some sort of surety, "All these people are around here to make a buck, and for every buck they make, a hundred others are trying to take it away from them."

Money has everybody on the prowl for a good deal. People ask, "how much?" as often as they say, "hello." In other words, money or its equivalent has been talking since the beginning of time and no one has been able to silence it. With the result that every time I walk into some clothing store, a salesman will try to put the kind of a suit on my back that will satisfy me well enough to prevent my going elsewhere. This merchant is not interested personally in whether I look like a reincarnation of Beau Brummell or the solidification of a ragpicker's dream, just as long as he makes a sale. And there are men standing behind merchandise counters today who would not leave a cash customer to himself, if their grandmothers were dying of convulsions in the next room.

We might say to some woman, "A mink coat would never make you happy" and although she would make big eyes and say, "Oh no!" the fact remains, it wouldn't. After a while her coat would become as commonplace and as ordinary as the parlor rug and she would find herself getting up in the morning with the same old chip on her shoulder, dreary at the thought of what the day might bring, hating to smile, hating even more the idea of being smiled at.

The old saying, "Money doesn't bring happiness" is true (although being an unhappy rich man would be better than being an unhappy poor man). Rarely is a man happy because of money itself. He might have it, but it isn't the money that brings him peace of mind or the knack of enjoying life. It is probably something else that didn't cost him a penny.

Still, life goes on, with making ends meet a perennial problem. And it will always be like that. Nothing will change it. Nothing, that is, save tearing yourself away from the whole circus. Nothing except getting out of the whole wild circle by kneeling at the altar and saying, "I promise poverty." Then life changes radically. Poverty becomes wealth.

We do not worry about paying bills because the majority of us never even see them. We can eat at our frugal tables without knowing the price of an egg. Our simple needs are provided by many kind souls who slip little white envelopes under our front door and then scurry back to the grind of getting a little something for themselves. No, we never realized how rich we could be until we took upon ourselves the life of poverty.

Probably the only real inconvenience in living a life of religious poverty is that which we call, "common property." This means that everything in the monastery belongs to everybody; and whatever one acquires for himself, he acquires for the community. For this reason the marking of clothes has become widespread among us. But mark as he will, a man never knows when he will lose his shirt. The brother in the next room has just as much right to it as anybody.

Even this is good. It breeds generosity. Poverty is like that. It is one of the greatest unifying forces in the world. Men of a common property share a common love. Their lack is mutual, and their mutual affection supports them in their need. No wonder the school of the apostles was a school of poverty. Their nothingness united them. And certainly Christ knew what it was to be poor. It was He who "had not whereon to lay His head," so He slept in the fields with the stars for a blanket. He begged His food. When He traveled, He walked. His was a life completely shorn of all luxury and His system worked. It still does.

As Carmelites we have received poverty as our heritage, from a foundress who was herself pre-eminently poor. St. Teresa loved poverty, and when food and clothing began coming through the turn with stern regularity, when she became deprived of deprivation, she felt as if she had lost "a great many golden trinkets."

And when things were not quite so miserably poor as usual, the nuns would say anxiously to Teresa, "Mother, we do not seem to be poor any more." They were not crazy; only different.

No, we are not rich. We never shall be, for we live by alms. It is a rather haphazard way of life, especially when a Loan Company asks for security, but it has always worked. And many times it is the poor old widow who in saying good-by palms a crumpled dollar bill in our hand. We know she needs it; we know she will feel its loss. But we also know that she needs far more than any dollar bill the tremendous blessings of God that will be hers because of her generosity.

So we friars don't worry if there is a hole in our pockets. What is wrong with a hole as long as there are no pennies to slip through? A hole in a pocket means the pocket is empty. And an empty pocket here on earth might possibly assure us a full pocket up in heaven.

❋ XIV ❋

No Wife

THERE is a strong element of surprise in chastity. A religious is surprised that he is able to take a vow of chastity; other people are surprised that he is able to keep it. But in spite of everything, chastity *is* possible. And it is entirely satisfying.

Certainly we religious bit off quite a mouthful when we decided that we were big enough to give ourselves to the service of the Church. We took vows. We promised poverty, realizing all the time that others without the vow would be far poorer than ourselves. We promised obedience knowing that no one is ever completely free from some kind of subservience. But when we promised chastity, we went far out on a limb and sat there before the gaze of a world that is intensely interested in the fact of the vow, but hardly able to understand it.

That is why any of us who has dealings with the laity finds himself at one time or another trying to give a good, sensible, and satisfactory answer to the old, old query, "Why don't religious marry?" We might get tired of this but we cannot lose our patience in the face of it. Whatever their reasons may be for asking, they still hold this of great importance. They cannot figure us out. And unless we come up with some good reasons for leading the kind of life we do, then many of us are going to find ourselves carrying through life the deep, indelible brand of "abnormal being."

I suppose the first and most salient reason for our choice is that Christ Himself lived a celibate life. We love Christ. Because we love Him, we try to make ourselves like Him in every respect. He is our model, so we strive to imitate Him not only in the things He chose to do, but also in the things He chose *not* to do. Christ lived a celibate life — this is good enough for us. There are other reasons but this is first. And even if there *were* no other reasons, this alone would be sufficient.

Getting along into the realm of practicality (and how the world loves that word "practical" — it is so broad), we find many good, solid reasons to give the person who asks "why?" First of all, saving souls is a full-time job. It occupies either directly or indirectly our every waking moment (and our dreams at night). Every single one of us is most definitely aware that in our life no other system could work. We cannot afford to shoulder obligations which by their very nature would take us away from our apostolate. We have enough to do as it is. Why, the wife of almost any good physician would tell us that her husband is more consistently a doctor than he is a husband or a father.

Now, in our particular community there are about thirty men who are completely taken up with saving souls — their own and others'. We live together in much peace and deep interior happiness. It is a man's world, in the strictest sense, because no woman may ever

enter our cloister. We are content here. True, we do get in one another's way sometimes. We do have our little disagreements (or I should say, differences of opinion) but far more often, we live untouched by the suffering and the loneliness that lie in thick, miasmic puddles outside our walls.

Just suppose that we were not bound to live a life of celibacy. Suppose we were all married men. That would automatically bring thirty women under our roof. And presuming that we would lead good Catholic lives, suppose we all had a family of five or ten children! We laugh to think of the intrigue, the confusion, the heartbreaking chaos that would surely descend upon our haven of prayer and work. Maybe this seems silly. Maybe it is no reason at all. But it certainly is something to think about. Maybe that is why some non-Catholic clergymen are beginning to embrace the celibate state. They are beginning to see that in laboring for God, it is the only thing that works.

Yet, people who are forced to lived in the fiery midst of a carnal world still look askance at us when we go by. Many question us and our motives, probably because they could not live like this themselves. And they harbor doubts because they have overlooked the battering but soothing dynamism that is the grace of God. They have forgotten that God's love has the power to make every burden light.

We do not say it is easy. But when we pluck the cross from the little Calvarys within our hearts, there is method to it. We are not seeking comfort or personal satisfaction, because there is no room for that in God's plan for us. So we turn our heads forward and upward, comprehending full well the enormity of our task. We must live and work in the midst of others' suffering, so we do not wish to be without suffering ourselves. In our labors we must come face to face with the full-cupped loneliness of men. We do not want to be without loneliness ourselves. We want to walk unafraid and un-ashamed at the side of those who need us and to be able to say, "You have suffering, so have we. You have loneliness, so have we. But we shall forget our problems; let us turn to yours. Let us heal yours, for ours can wait for eternity."

Yes, we are human but we have chosen to swerve from the tendencies of a human nature. We have not bucked nature; we have only tried to rise above it. We have not deprived ourselves of love; we have only found a greater. We have not hated the world; we have only loved something else more. In fact, the only love that we can permit ourselves is a love for God, a love that gives greater glory to Him, a love that takes in all nations, all creeds, all colors — everybody.

Our vow of chastity has not narrowed us, but rather it has made us take the whole world to ourselves. Maybe mankind will never understand us. But that fact doesn't change anything. Our vow has raised us to the point where we are able to look with sympathy and under-standing upon the souls who have become the victims of sin.

We have heard lay people say, "If I had my life to live over again, I would have become a religious." But we have never once heard a religious say, "If I had my life to live over again, I would have married." All of which gives us to believe that, however tough the vow of chastity (and religious life in general) may be, everyone seems to admit that in choosing to follow the ways of the Lord, we have chosen, by far, the better part.

❋ XV ❋

No Say

RELIGIOUS life can easily be a heaven on earth; but only for the man who lives it perfectly. And although much has been written on the fine art of acquiring perfection, all spiritual writers seem to agree on one big point. If a religious can obey, he can find perfect happiness. If he cannot obey, then he only nails himself to his own cross (by his own hand) and hangs forever on the left side of Christ. Religious life demands greatness; and a man is never greater than when he bows his head in submission to another.

Obedience is the big vow. Obedience is the problem. In our monasteries we are not free to do what we want, or have what we like. We are pledged to obedience and there is a solemn vow to remind us of it. It is a vow that makes us say "yes" when we would like to say "no." But when we take this vow, we offer to God one of our most priceless possessions: our free will. It is a perfect gift, one that God would never force from us. It is the last word, the limit. When we give this, we give everything. But it is only too bad that its worth is lost to many young men who, possessing all the other needed talents and dispositions, find themselves balking at what they call, "this business of taking orders."

These young men are legion. Any one of them might say, "Religious life is O.K., but I couldn't stomach the regimentation. I couldn't stand taking orders" (presupposing, I imagine, that we who take orders just love it). He is an interesting person. He thinks that we who have the vow of obedience would not even brush our teeth without a personal directive from Rome. Yet, he is a paradox.

He can't stand regimentation but no one is more regimented than he. He rises the same time every morning, arrives at his office on the dot, does the same work at the same desk year in and year out, goes home with the same crowd, eats the same set of suppers and watches the same run of TV shows. No he can't stand regimentation. Yet, the only break in the humdrum sameness of his life comes with summer vacation, when he spends two weeks either at the seashore or in the mountains. He is a slave to routine without even realizing it.

"I can't take orders," and although he thinks he means it, he forgets that there are some two hundred and forty-five senior members in his firm, all of them with enough authority to dump orders in his lap (which they do) — and he says he can't take orders. It is all he ever does. He takes orders from his parents and relatives. He takes orders from the lifeguard and the traffic cop. A million people run his life and he thinks he can be his own boss.

Actually, there is probably not a single man on the face of this earth who is free from the obligations of taking orders. Every subject has a boss who in turn has a boss, who in turn has another boss. It is the same in both lay and clerical circles. So we men in a monastery figure that since we must take order from someone, we might just as well make a good thing of it. We might just as well gain merit for our troubles.

Never having been a superior myself, I am tempted to let down the boom on superiors. But I can't, because I find nothing wrong with the system. Furthermore, we have a big change every three years, and that takes care of any problems that might arise. Every three years the new Prior comes to the monastery, assembles us in choir, and addresses us. His talk, like the talks of all new superiors, runs something like, "My dear brothers. God has chosen me to lead you for the next three years. I am not worthy of this and I am sure that any one of you could do a better job. But I only hope that we can all work together for God. Co-operation will maintain the happy atmosphere that has always been, I know, a part of this monastery." Then we go up, one by one, and offer him a fraternal embrace. After all, his words though well worn and often used before, are true. Co-operation does it. He might be a plain sort of a person but his heart is good. So everything will be perfectly all right.

Yes, everything *will* be all right. When a man spends about thirteen years in a monastery, he gets to know a little about superiors. When we were younger, we thought that being a superior was all tea and crumpets. We thought it was a soft job to sit down at a desk and give the orders. We decided, after suffering a rude squelch, that we would be different, we would do a

better job when we were in the saddle. But the years
teach a great lesson.

The human element in man might not always permit
us to agree with our superiors because, as individuals,
we all look at a situation in our own pigheaded way. But
we must admit that the superior has a hard job. The
troubles that come in the front door never reach us.
He is always there to intercept them and to shift them
to his own back. He must make the decisions. He must
sit up late at night and worry. He must be responsible
for the food that goes on our table each day. He must
clothe us. And when abuse rears its ugly head, he,
being the number one man, must smash it even though
he might be forced to suffer the passing chagrin of
some of his subjects. And this hurts him. A man rarely
likes to correct or admonish.

It is far more comfortable to mix with the common
crowd and agree or disagree with the way things are
being done. It is far easier to sit at the table and eat
the same amount of food each day without having to
worry about the prevailing high cost of living. In the
face of a horrible dilemma, we can leave the decision up
to the superior. If it is the wrong decision, he must take
the blame. If it is the right decision, we all reach out
for a share of the glory.

But this is not meant to give the impression that
obedience is easy. We who live within its holy clutch
know it is not. But this does not frighten us or give us
reason for complaint. After all, it was obedience that
put Christ on His cross. It might just as easily do it
to us.

Indeed, it is not always easy to agree with authority, holy as it is. It hurts to hear someone say, "Here's your transfer. Be out in three days." It is rather difficult to whisper a gentle, "I will," when everything inside is screaming, "I won't." It is also disconcerting (if we are foolish enough to worry about it) to pass one day never knowing where we will be tomorrow, never knowing what the next job will be, or when. But then, the whole thing strikes us as being so Christlike. "He went down and was subject to them." Can we do less?

Obedience is also sound wisdom. We can yell all we want about the hardships of obedience, but nothing can erase the corresponding privileges that go with it. It is our own unique satisfaction to know that every time we obey a superior, we obey the God who acts and speaks through him; every time we do the things that are commanded us, we are doing the things that God wants us to do.

There are many people today who are lost for the want of light to see God's will in their regard. Many of them would give their right arm (and cut it off themselves with a blunt knife) if they could discover positively what God wants of them. We do not have doubts like this. Our road is all light and security. In the will of our superior rests the will of God. And it doesn't matter if our superior is tall or short, slim or stout, round or square — when he speaks, God speaks. Our submission to him is our submission to God.

So we come and we go when we are told. We do what we are told and we do it as well as we can.

Some people might call us lifeless machines without

incentive, without personal push, or without a mind of our own. But pity the man of initiative, or with a mind of his own that is not in conformity with the mind of God. Yes, we might be spiritual robots with our own self-will immersed in the will of another. But because the distorted indulgence of self-will has been the frequent cause of eternal damnation right down from the time of Lucifer, then for better or worse, I think we'll take superiors. Obedience is so much safer.

❧ XVI ❧

Where Is the Page?

IN THE dining room of every Carmelite monastery there is an execution block. It does not take lives, but it does bring about progressive loss of weight as well as the incipient stages of nervous disorders. It is an enclosed dias, recessed into the wall, containing an oversized milking stool and a lectern. It is here that young clerics must read to the community during meals.

The idea of reading at meals is a good one. It is an ancient practice which has been universally adopted by practically all religious communities. For in the type of life that is given over to self-sanctification and the fostering of the higher faculties, this business of eating, although necessary, could easily become a great waste of time. So during meals, reading has been provided, with the hope that the friars will grow mentally as well as physically, thereby enabling them to provide for their minds with the same astute facility with which they provide for their stomachs.

It is difficult, however, to know just how to approach this thing — whether from the point of view of him who reads or of him who listens. Both parties have legitimate gripes; for as valuable as it may be, refectory reading is hard on everybody.

Take the young man who finds himself upon the stool, horribly alone and in the spotlight of men's minds. First of all, he knows as he rambles, that the best pieces of fish are being snared from the platters and all the sliced bananas are being skimmed off the top of the pudding. And when he does finish his given chore, he knows that he will have to dole out to himself a chilled bowl of soup, a dried-out lump of haddock, and the thick, hard hearts of the cabbage. But this is not all. The fact that he must read so as to be heard above the incessant cacophony of clattering knives and forks or falling dishes, this is the misery of it. To be clearly understood by the critical priests who, forfeiting the pleasures of their palate, concentrate all their attention upon the pure enunciation and intelligent delivery of the reader, this is the murder of it. So he stumbles. The harder he tries, the higher goes his voice. The more effort he expends, the faster comes his delivery. In no time at all, he has completely discounted the value of articles and conjunctions (all small words, in fact) and has ended by shoving them all together into one great vocal ball, and casting it willy-nilly upon the air. With the result that "as it was" comes out "ezwuz" and the statement "all kiss the floor" sounds much like "August the four." In a frenzy he finishes, then stumbles down the steps, glides across the slippery floor and piles himself into a huge brown wreck before the relentless advance of the creaking dish wagon. He hates reading.

But when he concludes, we relax too. A deep calm covers the room. The high velocity bleatings of a confused Brother are stilled, and we turn to our coffee in gratitude. We are the ones who must sit and listen, so we are glad when it is all over. We resolve, therefore, to better the situation by gently laying a fatherly hand upon the boy's shoulder and saying, "Look, son, your reading is abominable. But so was ours. Read slower, pronounce *all* the words, not half of them. If an author used a preposition, he had a reason for it. He wants you to read it. And take your time. We have no deadlines. When we finish this book, we have a thousand more. But we don't care about them, only the one we are reading now."

To you Brothers who read in our refectories, we have some questions for you. What happens to all the bookmarks which are there one day but gone the next? Who has filched them? Or has someone eaten them? And when you *do* find another bookmark, why must you so place it that we are forced to listen to the same stuff three or even four times over? Again, when you are not shouting, why must you whisper? Even when we cock our raised cowls behind our ears, we still cannot hear you.

Is the vision of many friars smiling into their food, lulled by the gentle but firm voice of an intelligent reader — is this all a pipe dream? Will we ever have readers, who through the mellifluousness of their voices will so capture our minds that the food grows cold before us?

I wager "no," because the way things are now, they always were. And we who are officially deputized to correct and remedy, we can point out the errors and the mistakes, but we don't kid ourselves. We were the same when we were clerics. I suppose that a fearless, clear, although strident voice comes with maturity. I suppose it is something that one must grow up to. Just like sanctity.

But all we ask of you who read (and it is small) is that the next time you get up to fulfill your office, don't say, "Being chapter orr." Say, rather, "The beginning of Chapter Four" and go on from there. Keep us happy, you who read to us. Calm our nerves, give us rest, let our souls be peaceful. So that when dinner is over we may go to our recreation room in a gentle frame of mind.

≫XVII≪

Fish Is a Problem

WHEN I signed my name on the dotted line and became a Discalced Carmelite, it was taken for granted that I understood all the privileges and obligations that were bound up in that specific vocation. Certainly I knew what the holy vows entailed. I understood the legislation of the Order in the matter of silence, retirement, and mortification. I realized that my life was pre-eminently a life of contemplation and that even if I never went into a pulpit, I would have no reason to complain. At that time they told me about midnight office and I nodded my head up and down like a dummy. They told me about the two hours of daily mental prayer and I took it unflinchingly like a martyr of old. But when they told me that the all-important item of meat was scratched off the diet, I softly wilted, and took it as a necessary evil. If I wanted the full richness of Carmel, I had to take it in its entirety, and not part here and part there. So when I signed my name on the dotted line, I blandly disregarded my taste buds and joined.

The question of who eats all the fish that are caught could probably best be answered by some Economic Security Control, which could back up its pronounce-

ments with an impressive array of figures and statistics. All I can say is that Carmelites must eat most of it. Day in and day out fish *sans* head and tail are set out on our tables. It comes fried, roasted, broiled, baked, and curried; but it never loses its identity. It is always just what God meant it to be: fish.

Four hundred and fifty pounds of it will fit into our deep freeze. All sizes, shapes, and colors fill our refrigerator. We have it every day, all year round, and when Thanksgiving comes, we have fish for dinner.

Yes, I suppose there are some people in this crazy world who like fish, but we have all met those who die a death every Friday when they are forced to rely on sea food for sustenance. Certainly there is only one reason why we hold to this diet. It is not by reason of thrift, because somewhere along the line the common species of fish picks up a value almost comparable to that of beef. Nor is it by reason of health alone that we eat fish. Good vitamin pills are better. Carmelites have been eating fish for centuries for the stark, simple purpose of doing penance. We eat fish to atone for our own sins and for the sins of the world.

We eat it for the same reason that Catholics eat it every Friday to suffer in some small way because Christ suffered on a Friday. Back in the days of pagan Rome, Friday was set aside by the people as the day for their weekly gorge. We try to make up to God for this ancient abuse. In fact, this ancient abuse is not so very ancient. It is about as old as last night's paper.

We eat fish every day in that spirit of simplicity which was always such an integrated part of the life of Christ.

Fish for the most part is a poor man's food. We too are poor. Furthermore, we offer to God this voluntary sacrifice of a meatless diet with the sincere hope that He will send saintly and ever more numerous priests into the world.

We accept this penance as we accept every other penance, not because we enjoy it but rather because it hurts. Usually the things that hurt most are the things that are most pleasing to God. No one ever made advance in perfection by constantly doing the things he liked or avoiding the things he did not like. So we eat fish because it is a sacrifice and because it is something hard.

Indeed, we are not complaining about what appears on our dishes each day. But we do feel rather drained when we meet the occasional woman who, in what she thinks is a flash of brilliant originality, says to us: "My John should have been a Carmelite. He just loves fish." True, he can really go to work on a big Maine lobster drenched in melted butter. He is really mad about the deviled crabs that he picks up on Saturday nights at the local tavern. And oysters and cherry-stone clams are his constant delight. Yes, "My John should be a Carmelite. He just loves fish." But if John ever did become one of us, he would find out the very same thing I did. Just for the record, in all the thirteen years I have worn the garb of the Order I love, I can recall having fried oysters about ten times, lobster three times, and the left leg of one frog. Yes, of fish, John can have my share. I'll take potatoes.

❧XVIII❧

Are Your Feet Cold?

Brother COSMO swings a merry hammer when it is time to make a sandal. His environment is not exactly a monument to the cobbler's art but years of religious life have taught him to make the best of everything. The monastery shoe shop is usually buried in the deepest corner of the lowest basement where its pitifully inadequate machinery is rooted squarely between a huge, grizzly washing machine and a cluttered carpenter's bench. It is designated as a place where Brother may work in his sporadic moments of free time.

Now when Cosmo has got himself a bit caught up on his many other duties, he dons his blue denim apron, draws his last and other needed accessories around him, fills his mouth with shoe nails, and goes to work. All alone, with the quiet determination and grim fortitude of a great artist, he takes leather, glue, and tacks, breathes order into the confusion, and when he arises from his stained and discarded piano stool, he has created a sandal.

Sandals are his business and he is proud of his craft. But no worldly wise shoemaker would even attempt to do what Brother Cosmo does. His is a devil-may-care product, a thing of rugged, austere beauty which has

evolved from years of persistent effort and at the cost of much trial and error. The only question in his mind as he settles himself for the job is, "What size shoe do you wear?" God help us!

Now, just for the record, Discalced Carmelites did not always wear sandals. Years ago, they simply went without any footwear at all. Indeed, the word "discalced" means "barefooted," "unshod." Why they reverted to the wearing of sandals nobody really seems to know. Perhaps they discovered that wearing sandals oftentimes involved greater penance than not wearing them. Or perhaps again, there were a lot of colds going around. Suffice it to say that sandals, as we have them today, are the most recent form of penance that have been added to the holy habit.

A sandal is something made to "sort of" fit the foot. It makes little difference whether a monk's toe hangs over the front of the sole, or his heel protrudes over the back. It makes little difference also if his feet happen to swish around in the wide freedom of an oversized piece of hide. The only requisite is that the sandal go along with the man. As for a definition, probably all that can be said is, "a slab of 'neolite,' with straps running over the instep and around the heel, fastened by a buckle or a collar button." This is undoubtedly vague, but so is the whole business. And because the sandal is not made for comfort, a monk has no complaint when Cosmo drops another finished product on his bed.

After the first few years of his monastic life, a man stops wondering and worrying about his sandals. He takes them for granted. But the outsider doesn't. The monastery in itself holds a strong fascination for the ordinary layman. And a friar is always eager to impart to others the glory and the marvel of his life. He is only too happy to tell people about Carmelite prayer. He is anxious to explain the vital importance of contemplation in today's world. He is ever ready to point out the good that comes from penance and the rich acquisitions of soul that come through holy silence. He will relate with delight the story of the brown scapular he wears. But when he is approached by inquisitive lay people, do they ask him about contemplation? Do they ask him to teach them how to pray? Do they want to learn the happy, positive side of mortification? Are they interested in the history of the Order or the story of Mary's scapular? No, none of these! They only approach him while a lusty wind blows in from the north and they ask, "Say, Father, are your feet cold?"

This, then, is the question. How to answer it! Let us suppose that I stand out on the road with the mercury flirting with freezing point. Are my feet cold? Let me put it this way. If your uncovered hands are cold, then my feet are cold. But if you find it comfortable enough to go without gloves, then I find it comfortable enough to go without shoes. Pointedly, our feet are *not* cold. We have accepted bare feet as we have accepted bare faces. We like the wind blowing among our toes. We think it is healthful. We like our sandals, and our feet are not cold. A man can get used to anything.

Not that this type of footgear does not have drawbacks. It does. Let a man wear sandals continuously over a period of years and his feet begin to go flat. His arches begin to fall. Eventually, like Lil Abner, he finds difficulty in getting into a pair of conventional shoes. Furthermore, unless he keeps his sandals under his pillow all night, he will find them very cold and harsh on his bare feet in the morning. And when winter is at its worst the skin around his heel will crack and painfully open. If a man is strong he will rely on the ordinary healing powers of nature. If he is a chicken, he will strike out for the infirmary and a band-aid. But even with all this, we still like our sandals.

When Christ came to earth, He came as a poor man. He traversed the roads in poverty and like all poor men of the time, he wore sandals. Certainly if they were good enough for Christ, then they are good enough for us. So we wear them.

And all the time we are quite conscious of those who dress up their feet in the warmest and most comfortable manner. We are also conscious of certain of the men who have come out of Korea on stretchers, and who will need never worry about footwear again, because they have no feet. They have no legs. So we are satisfied to be the unshod of the Lord. We are supremely content to go through life with flapping sandals. For many things in this world do not matter very much. And comfortable feet are among them.

❯❯ XIX ❮❮

As All Men Must

OUR new cemetery had not been blessed very long
before it took into its rocky, earthen bosom — a friar.

Old Brother Jude had worked hard to make the place
a fitting haven for the dead. He had laid the whole
thing out by himself down in the valley behind the
Seventh Station. He had cleared the land, removed the
tree stumps, made paths, planted grass, and then put a
fence around it. Then he eyed the community. Seeing
a couple of old priests daily growing riper and riper
for heaven, he went down and covered a portion of the
lot with a thick, warm layer of straw. If he had to dig
a grave during the winter, the straw would keep the
ground from freezing and make his job a whole lot
easier. It was a wise move because that winter we did
need a grave. But it wasn't Brother Jude who dug it.
We dug it. Brother Jude went into it. And this is just
about as close as anyone comes to digging his own
grave.

Some people say that the only thing wrong with
dying is that you are dead so long. To such people death
is the absolute end of everything. But we who live in
a monastery are keenly aware of the words of Christ,
"He who believes in Me, even if he die, shall live; and

whoever lives and believes in Me shall never die." We are convinced of the truth of this.

When we put away one of our own, there is some strange element, either added or subtracted, which changes things. There is no futility there, no hopelessness, no frustration over the thought that one we love will never walk through our corridors again. In other words, death does not hurt so much. Probably the only reason for our entering a monastery in the first place is to die well. And when we die well, then we have accomplished our purpose. No one is selfish enough to hope that we might be deprived of an eternal reward in exchange for a few more years' reprieve on this earth. We are here because there is a God and a heaven. This is what keeps us going. This is what gives sanction to our lives. For if there were no God or no heaven, then, truly, we would all be crazy to live as we do.

I was only a young student when death struck among us for the first time in my religious life. Father Hilary was breathing his last. Having borne with us during his life, he had a right to our presence at the moment of his death. So at the sound of the bell we gathered in the infirmary to recite the prayers that would send him on his way. Many of the community assembled for this as they assembled for any other exercise. Nothing very unusual about it. Friars had been dying for centuries. Their deportment was prevaded with manliness. Watching them, I thought to myself. "These men are rugged. They might be soft on the inside, but they are hard on the outside. Their hearts might be as gentle as the heart of Christ, but their spirits are as inflexible as tempered steel." That is why, while we knelt and prayed, the cook was worrying about the soup boiling over, and the porter was afraid that he might not hear the phone ring amid the recitation of the prayers for the departing. And all the others, with the peaceful passivity that comes from a lifelong resignation to God's will, kept the prayers going, satisfied to get them finished, to let Hilary die, so they could all get back to their respective duties.

We neophytes reacted differently. For most of us this was the first time that we had seen death. So we looked hard at Father Hilary. What does it feel like to die? Up until the time of his sickness, Father Hilary had been teaching us philosophy. He believed that because God created man, body and soul, these two elements should never have been separated. Sin changed this; sin demanded such a separation. So Father Hilary was convinced that when the soul left the body at death, the separation was for a brief instant a tearing, ruthless thing. Of death he had no fear; of the separation, this is what puzzled and worried him. Now, at last, he had discovered what it was like. His searching was over. Now he knew. In apparent peace he departed the earth with the holy oils heavy on his body — as ready as anyone could ever hope to be.

One minute he was a priest, a brilliant scholar, teacher, linguist, a saint. The next minute he was a corpse just like any other corpse. So we put his remains into the hands of our "family" undertaker, who gave it the same treatment reserved for all cadavers, saints and sinners alike.

Father Hilary was waked in the great monastery church with two friars in constant attendance at the bier. I drew the midnight watch along with a classmate, Brother Reginald. Neither of us liked the idea of being alone at night in a big empty church with a dead body, but when the time came, we went bravely out to relieve two lay brothers. These were hardened men, long in the Order, realists, not given to emotional spasms, masters of life and future masters of their own deaths. As we got on our knees beside them, they hoisted themselves to their feet, walked over to the side of the simple black coffin and looked down into the face of Father Hilary. Any ideas we might have had about their saying a final silent prayer for the deceased were blanketed when one of them, eyeing the well-groomed beard, gave it a gentle tug and whispered, "I wanted to do that all my life." Then they went to bed.

The lay brothers educated us that night. They gave us the right idea. So we remained motionless where we knelt, enthralled over the simplicity and reality of death. Death became, then, a very uncomplicated thing, a phase of existence, a change, but nothing really to get excited about.

On the day of the funeral we put Father Hilary away right, and gave him everything that a priest, as well as our brother, deserves from those he leaves behind. But there were no tears. Appreciation, yes! Gratitude for what he had done, yes! But the Provincial was not forced to remove his glasses during the sermon to avoid getting them all steamed up. It was all very sensible. After Mass the coffin was closed and the body taken down behind the Seventh Station. We formed a circle and recited the final prayers. The only disturbances were the antics of the Thurifer, who was swinging his thurible in violent, giant parabolas trying to keep a good fire going, and the efforts of a young friar, who was practically walking on heads trying to get some good snapshots of a coffin with its gaping hole beneath.

Then Father Hilary went down jerkily into his grave. The lay brothers did not waste any time covering the rough box. With the sound of soil pounding down upon a coffin, we went back to our cloister. How would we manage to get along without Father Hilary? He was a big man, an able man, the kind of person not easily replaced. But we should have known better. Sure, we lost a good teacher. Sure, they had to remove from his confessional the sign that informed penitents of his ability to hear confessions in eight languages. But religious life is not the least bit affected by the disappearance of men. For the life is inviolable. Men will die; others will take their places. We are all expendable.

Back in the monastery, dinner was a feast. Silence was dispensed, so during the meal we celebrated. Yes, Father Hilary was gone. So would we be some day. But now it was ours to enjoy the reunion of old friends and classmates brought together again at the cost of a friar's death. We did not cry. We laughed. We celebrated on account of Father Hilary. For he had found what all of us were still searching for. He had found God.

Rough Hands

EVERY time someone picks up a ringing phone in the monastery, he is trained to say, "Good morning, Carmelite Fathers," whether he is actually a Father or not. It is a wonder people haven't taken issue with this by some statement like "What have they got there besides Fathers?" It would be a good question. The title, "Discalced Carmelite Fathers" is retained and carried through our every contact with the outside world. It is found on our writing paper, in legal documents, in Catholic directories, in telephone books. Yes, it is a *very* good question: "What have they got there besides Fathers?"

Well, besides students, we have Brothers (sometimes referred to as Lay Brothers but there is nothing "lay" about them). The whole purpose of their life is to keep the wheels turning in the monastery. Chances are, if a man knocks on our front door, it will be a Brother who admits him. What about these men whom we talk about so little and yet need so much?

They are men who come from the same kind of a home that priests come from. They studied from the same books; played the same games. And they entered the Order to save their own souls and to help in the salvation of others by the specific work assigned them.

The Brother turned down the priesthood not because he could not master the studies, not because he could not preach or teach, and certainly not because he did not love the idea of saying Mass. He became a Brother because he knew that God did not want him to become a priest. It is as simple as that.

Here in the monastery, preaching to his fellow religious by his good example, doing the more menial tasks so that priests and students might be free to pursue their studies — this is his vocation. Humility is his specialty. And although he is not a servant or a valet but a full sharer in all the privileges of the Order, still he is the man who teaches young religious many useful

tricks, and then sits back in his same old place and watches them grow up to become his superiors.

His life is the life of Nazareth, the life of hidden work and hidden meaning, lived behind the veil of his unselfishness, shielded from the eyes of men; but strong and rich in its purpose because it is lived not for any reward here on earth but for God alone.

We men who are priests today can never forget our wonderful associations with the Brothers. They have taught us many things. And when the work was hard, it was their own dogged persistence and kind encouragement that made us pick up the shovel again for another try. In our student days we viewed the sky from the bottom of many a deep, freshly dug hole. And on those occasions when we stood down there in the pit, sweating from every pore, with loose dirt slithering down our backs and into our work shoes; when we were all ready to burrow into the side of the hole where we might rest forever in the bosom of rock and soil, it was the Brother who would say, "Lets dig, friends, the bottom can't be much farther."

And when we helped the Brother in the kitchen, we didn't do the professional work that he did. We only scraped the grease-covered pans beneath the burners of the stove, or washed the pots. Any little thing, just to give him a break. And when we left, tired, smelly, and glad to get out, we figured, "Well, he's still in there and he won't get out until they roll him out."

We don't know how many debts we owe to a Brother for the press job he put into pants, or the snaps and buttons he sewed on our habits or our shirts. I cannot remember ever having darned my socks; but somebody darned them. Sure, it was the Brother. We owe him for the way he pampered us in the past, and for all the times he tolerated with a smile our inabilities to do the things he did so well himself. And he never griped because we were so thick and useless. He just went ahead and filled the need.

These are the things that make us proud of our Brothers, things that are so commonplace but necessary — and for which we have forgotten to say thanks. But the point is, these Brothers do not wait for or expect the kind of thanks that we could give them. If they did, they would wait a long time. We are guilty of the sin of taking all this for granted, for being the object of such genuine, positively needed attention without which we could not work; yet, failing to appreciate fully, or even partially sometimes, the love and selflessness that went into their work. So we put on our sackcloth, kneel down in the ashes, and chant our *Miserere* to atone for our crime of "getting used to the Brothers."

Even as I write this the faint aroma of food comes in through my window telling my nose that the cook is on the job and that dinner will be ready on schedule. Downstairs, too, across from the kitchen, the sewing machine is purring and another habit for some priest is getting its final shakedown. In a few moments the phone will ring again and another Brother will take the receiver from its cradle and say, "Good morning. Carmelite Fathers. . . . No, I'm not a priest; I'm a Brother. . . . Yes, I *know* that's no help to you but I'm satisfied to be what I am. Just wait one minute and I'll call a priest. You can talk to him. . . . No, it's no trouble at all. It's my job and I'm happy to do it. Hang on a minute."

Yes, he's quite a guy, our Brother. He is oil for the wheels and fuel for the fire of our monastery. He is life to Carmel. But when he goes to bed at night there are no cheering crowds to praise his work. Only God is his witness. But whether at home or in foreign fields, his hands, consecrated by labor, are bent to the task of the great harvest. That is why his place in heaven will probably be higher than our own. God knows, he certainly deserves it.

⁂ XXI ⁂

The Lowly Vow

SUNK deeply here in the middle of this book are a few words on the subject of the fourth vow that all Discalced Carmelites take along with the other three — the vow of humility.

Once upon a time, a very brilliant gentleman wrote: "We have learned to fly the skies like birds and to swim the seas like fish; now we need only learn how to walk the earth like men." And there is much that could be said about that.

Man is a very capable animal. Yet, with all his abilities, he steps forth upon the stage of life as the greatest paradox of God's creation. He can achieve so much at one time, so little at another. He can make himself so sublime and yet, at times, so ridiculous. He is possessive of the highest, noblest forms of heroism, still he can sink himself into the deepest pits of cowardice. Nor do we know exactly how to change or remedy this.

But we do believe that if a man turned more often to God with a nod of thanks for what he is and for what he has, he would be a far better man. If he became more God-centered and less self-centered, if he stopped thinking he was a saint in his own right, but rather bore witness to his own sinfulness, he would more easily

become in fact, the saint he thinks he is.

So in order to destroy within us any vestige of that pride which is an abomination to God, the Church and the Order demand of us this fourth vow. This vow, of course, does not make us perfectly humble the moment we take it, but it tries. Nor does it immediately destroy all pride in our lives, but it tries that, too. The vow itself forbids our ever seeking any honors above that of the simple priest. And it is a good idea. It takes all the politics out of politics. It lifts us above the blight of subtle connivance and gentle intrigue. Then when election time comes, no one can do any lobbying, no one can do any pushing or pulling — with the result that the Holy Spirit is left entirely free to go about His work of inspiration. Our vow cannot condone any such promise as, "You vote for me and I will provide for you." Therefore, when our superiors are chosen, we know it is the work of God and not of men.

I do not mean to infer by this that there are politics in religious life. Let us say that the vow was instituted not to destroy an abuse but to prevent one. One can never tell what will happen in the future. But perhaps in centuries to come, some little friar in some little monastery on the other side of the world might get a little political, a little ambitious. Hence, the vow.

Humility, as we accept it by profession, tries to lead us up the mountain of virtue. It makes us tremendously aware of what we are — not much even at our best. It gives us an insight into one of the greatest truths of our faith, that everything we have and are is the result of God's goodness. But just as He has every right to give us what He deemed proper, so has He the same right to take it away. And so, whatever good we can do for souls, we know it is the grace and love of God that enables us to do it. And whatever glory we might obtain upon earth is a glory that must be shared with Him who gave birth to it in the first place.

It is salutary to think about these things. We are all so prone to fall in love with ourselves. We are all so anxious to hear the praises that men might heap upon our heads. In this blindness we fail to realize that half the nice things that people say about us might easily be lies anyway. The other half, we do not deserve. We are only fooling ourselves when we lap all this up and pat ourselves on the back. We are only re-echoing, however unconsciously, the words of the Pharisee, *"O God, I give thanks that I am not as the rest of men. . . ."* How God must laugh at our stupidity. How He must shake His head and wonder where we ever got such ideas.

Yes, what has happened to the world's humility? Too often it has become a weakness in the eyes of men. It has been shunned and despised. But no amount of profound thinking on the part of the brilliant minds of scholars will ever make pride a virtue. No verbal distortion of facts will ever make humility a sin. And nothing will ever be able to change or erase the words that Christ spoke to His disciples, "Amen, I say to you, unless you be converted and become as little children, you shall not enter the kingdom of heaven. Whoever, therefore, shall humble himself — he is the greater in the . . . kingdom of heaven."

Priesthood

❊ XXII ❊

Forever

HOW long does it take to become a priest? Ten years? Twenty years? A thousand, perhaps? How many tears does a man shed? How many times does his muddled brain urge him to heave his books right out the window? How many times does he serve Mass itching to say it himself? Time solves it all. But who can measure yearning by a slide rule?

But one day toward the end of our studies, life began to quicken its tempo. Hardly perceptible at first, it flowered swiftly into the great actuality. We began saying "dry Masses" on the improvised altars. We began considering designs for chalices. We checked engravers for ordination announcements. Soon, so soon in fact, that we were almost caught spiritually unaware, we lay prostrate on the cold floor of our monastery chapel, waiting with singularly grateful hearts for the only thing in the world we ever really wanted. Then, in interior but controlled confusion, we knelt before the Archbishop, felt the imposition of his hands upon our heads, while for a fraction of time the world stood still. Then we returned to our places. Priests forever!

Any priest who tries to write about his ordination day suffers the grim danger of becoming effusively sentimental. Words might easily jeopardize or efface the things he knows and feels. He waits a few years before he talks about it. He comes down from the clouds, plants himself, surveys the situation, then evaluates his gift. He waits until the novelty is gone, until only the glow is left. And the glow is something that is always with him.

What is it like to be a priest? It is the fullness of living. It is everything. It is the thought that rushes through your mind at the most unlikely times, "I am a priest." It is the sensation of being needed when you break through the crowd that encircles a tragedy and hear people say, "Make way for the priest." It is the sound of a child's voice calling you "Father" and the earnestness of a young man who says, "I never told this to anyone but I'll tell it to you." It is the recognition of the stranger who tips his hat on the street. The reverence of the good nuns who, somewhat like taxidermists, are proud to "stuff" Father in their guest dining rooms. These are some of the good things that make the priesthood worth while. But even the hard things are no less challenging.

We found, as priests, that for every person who might listen to the word of God coming from our lips, there were twenty-five who wouldn't. We collided with reality. We saw people not as we would want them to be but as they actually are. So we found out at last why Christ wept over the old Jerusalem, because many times we felt like weeping over the new one ourselves. The true meaning of His words "I thirst" brought His thirst into our own lives. And before very long we understood that the greatest hardship that could come into our priestly lives was not loneliness, or privation, or personal failure; but rather the souls that we could not reach or save, souls that we could not bring to love God. Even in the crowds, seen from the corner of every eye, we were alone, looked upon more as museum pieces than as other Christs.

However, to many who do not accept the spiritual implications of our divine mission, we are received as doctors or lawyers are received — professional men, educated and trained in a specific science. To those who do accept us, we are received for what we are — other Christs and apostles of the Lord. To one another we are sharers in the great brotherhood of Catholic priests, a brotherhood that is too tender to be called fellowship and too sturdy to be called love. As for the rest, it is of little importance to us what people say or think about us. And to those who take a perverted sense of delight in tearing us down in seventy-two different ways, we can only say this in our defense (if a defense is necessary): When Christ came down upon this earth to begin His work of redemption, He chose twelve simple, ignorant, ordinary men on which to found His church. (And the true rock, Peter, was probably the most ignorant of them all.) Today, after all these years, Christ still chooses the same kind of men to carry on His work.

We priests therefore do the best we can. You have seen us angry sometimes and you condemned us for it, saying, "Christ was never like that"; but you didn't consider that we might have been sitting for three hours in a hot confessional with a bleeding ulcer, or that some kid had blooped a baseball through a stained-glass window. You saw us sad and you complained about our lack of an even disposition, but you forgot that we too have our hard days and that our hearts can also break at the sight of much good destroyed in minutes. And then, even when we laughed — long and hard as all men must at times — you pointed out to others our lack of dignity and reserve saying, "Father should realize his position."

You were shocked at the cars you saw us drive. You were positively intolerant of the radios in rectory rooms. But truthfully, would to God we did not have to have cars or radios. Would to God we could reach you and bring Christ into your lives without them. If it would do any good, we would sell those devices tomorrow. But then you would say, "Why doesn't Father stop being so old-fashioned? He should be out in the front leading rather than off in the back pushing."

No, maybe we cannot reach you all the time. But we try. That is why we wave as we walk down the street. That is why we lay our consecrated hands on the little heads of your children. Just so that you can see us. Just so that you know we are there and still going. And won't you say *"Hello, Father"* when you meet us? We like to know that *you* know we *are* your Father. It makes life so much easier for us.

Yes, we love you with a love that is as eternal as our priesthood. But maybe it will take heaven for you to understand that. And maybe you will find someday that you are in heaven because of the faltering efforts of some priest who, in giving his all, knelt each morning at his prie-dieu and prayed: "In peace is my bitterness most bitter." Up among the angels you will come to know the length and the depth of our devotion to your cause. It might take heaven itself to make you love us, as we, in Christ, have loved you. Yes, it might take heaven. For earth has not always done it.

To be a priest, to say Mass, to walk among you as Christ walked among you — this is our life. And although we may never be able to enrich your lives in any material way, we give you much more — the Body and Blood of Christ, the forgiveness of your sins, and an inside track on the path to heaven.

⚜ XXIII ⚜

Bless Me, Father...

THE priesthood can easily be for the man who possesses it the most thrilling and the most priceless experience in the world. This is what our retreat master told us on those days before our ordination. And during that retreat he made many promises. He told us that as long as we remained faithful to our calling as Carmelite priests, we would never know a day of real unhappiness in our lives. He assured us that although our acquisitions in the coin of men would be nil, our gain would be relegated to the riches of heaven. Above all, our retreat master impressed upon us the conviction that the most glowing jewel of our priesthood would be the gift of God's peace, in our souls, in our hearts, and in our minds.

I took notes during that retreat, and even if I could not decipher my scrawl, I know what they were supposed to mean. They are all there, those promises; and after some years as a priest I am still convinced that he wasn't just using platitudes. His words were true. I am forced to admit that even with the trifling inconveniences that must by force of circumstances come into any life, I had found the peace and the happiness he had promised.

119

But there was a day when I walked up and down the monastery corridor with my peace of mind torn and shattered. Its tiny pieces seemed to be cluttering up the floor where I walked. Shortly before that, slumped in my usual place at the bare table in the refectory, I had raised my eyes to see the Brother Porter enter and whisper with his usual barroom buzz into the Prior's ear, "Some people for confession."

Everybody heard it. But it didn't bother the others as it bothered me. That is why I quickly turned back to the orange in my hands and frantically whittled away at its speckled rind. "Jesus, Mary, and Joseph be my salvation . . . can this be *it?*" And it was. The Brother came over to me, bent down and mumbled, "Confessions, Father." Nothing like this had ever been spoken to me before. Were these my ears? Being called "Father" was enough, but confessions — saints preserve me! Nonplused is a mild word, but how else can I describe myself, as I left the room and walked up and down the corridor waiting for my first penitents to make their way into the chapel. Guinea pigs.

I paced and I reasoned. After all, I *had* received full faculties a few days before. And they *had* designated me a lawful confessor with "knowledge, uprightness, and prudence." All those years that went into the preparation for just this could not have been wasted years — the endless expanse of books assimilated, the lectures, the term papers, the examinations both written and oral. I could not know everything, but I had done my best in the classroom.

But the comforting thought of God reached out to

raise me up. He was Number One in this business while I was only His instrument. And God knew how to wield such instruments. But still, what if I became lost for the right words to comfort a needy soul? What if I forgot the form of absolution? What if this or that should happen? Suppose I get a reserved sin or a censure. How will I ever juggle it? Suppose there is a nun out there, or a priest. They're not going to like it. Good Lord, we've even had bishops in our confessional. Dear God, don't make it a bishop!

Of one thing I was certain. Nothing was going to shock me. During my course of Theology I learned about many sins and how they were committed. So I presumed that they were not just some theological flights of fancy but hard fact. All of us had become very broad-minded with a sense of understanding as big as the moon. Nobody was going to tell me anything new in that box. Nobody was going to surprise me.

On the way to the chapel, at last, I felt very conscious of my hands as I washed and dried them. They were just ordinary hands, I thought, as I looked at them. There was a scar on my left index finger, a childhood souvenir of my attempt to cut a hard little apple with a big, shiny knife. And down in the palm of the same hand was a rather ugly scar, another memento of a little boy's losing battle with an automobile. The thumb of my left hand gave indication of the time I had cut it to the bone on the sharp edge of a coffee can; with another finger of that hand bearing some small blemish of a forgotten origin. Otherwise, they were ordinary hands. But in a few short moments these same hands would operate to wash away sin and conquer evil, for that was the design of God. Someday God would judge me by those hands. He would say from His judgment seat, "Let me see your hands, Father." And with them I would judge myself.

I slipped quietly out the door into the chapel. Briefly, I knelt before Christ, and asked Him to judge my first penitents as well as those who would follow them. I asked him to fill my heart with His own mercy, His own meekness and kindness, and finally, to make me in some way worthy of this awful honor. For I was a sinner like all men. Who was *I* to judge *them?*

Getting off my knees, I headed for the confessional — a brand new trip, a journey I had never taken before. Arriving, I opened the door, and angry at myself for not having looked this situation over before, I felt around for the chair and the stool. I sat down in the darkness. Probably every young priest feels terribly alone at that moment. There are no books to consult. There are no sharp professors to come up with the right answers. No coaxing. Just you, all by yourself. Isolated.

But here the poignancy of the priesthood becomes vivid and most real. That very morning I had taken a host into my hands and changed it into the Body and Blood of Christ. I could not see any change. I could not feel any. But in the confessional things would be different. Here I would deal with the bodily presence of sinners and through them, the physical, sensible reaction of the working of God's grace among men. In them I would see the elation at having thrown off the bonds of sin, the joy of receiving courage to begin life anew, the gratitude expressed in mumbled thanks through the screen.

There would be the tears of men who sinned and then wept because they did. All this would be sufficient reward for the long hours that I might spend under the constant dronings of human frailty — the same old sins committed in the same old way under the same old circumstances. There would be nothing new, nothing that had not been confessed before. But always the freshness of a new purification and a new start, the change to begin again to live in grace and to prepare for death.

I thought of all this as I sat there in the blackness. Now I would exercise a newly acquired power. It had been passed on to me by my predecessors — this strange power that made Christ ever victorious over the power of hell. Now I would do what comparatively few men could do — annihilate sin. Through countless years men who betrayed Christ had fought to throw off the stain of their betrayal; they had agonized to stifle the remorse that gripped their souls; they had writhed in the pressing force of guilt which possessed them. But they could not win. They could not free themselves. Only a priest could do that.

So I took a deep breath, pulled back the slide, put my ear to the screen — and softly it came: "Bless me, Father, for I have sinned."

⇜ XXIV ⇝

I Pity Teachers

I PITY teachers because once I was one myself. And all the while I was, I pitied myself. It is not that I have any ax to grind with teaching itself; but I do feel that my appearance upon the scholastic podium has set the profession back about thirty years.

I could not explain why I was made a teacher any more than I could explain the dynamic principles of social rehabilitation (if there are such things). God did it to me; it was all His fault.

But this much I know. When I was a boy, God blessed me with a priestly vocation. I set out to find the Order which suited me by using the process of elimination. I was *not* going to be a teacher. I knew the Jesuits and their world-wide interest in all things academic. I saw the Oblates of Saint Francis trying to put some order into the plus-4000 boys who crowded the halls of North Catholic High in Philadelphia. I sat beneath the eyes of the Christian Brothers and boldly flunked a scholarship exam. All these men, in my mind, personified the classroom. So I turned and walked no more with them.

In Carmel I found what I was looking for. Here (I figured) was an Order in which I could live a life of prayer and at the same time enjoy an occasional opportunity to preach the word of God. So I became a Carmelite. When I became a priest, the superior called me into his room one day and asked, "Father, have you any special interests? What would you like to do?"

"Father Provincial," I answered, "it is not for me to say what I would like to do. But I will tell you what I would *not* like to do. I would *not* like to teach."

Which seemed to be all right with him because for one grand year, and only one, I was spared what I feared most.

It was a strange, difficult year. People would ask me what kind of work I did. "O, I just lead the community life in the monastery, follow the bells and pray for the world." But the answer never seemed to jell in the minds of my interested listeners. "Yes, but what do you *do?*" All year I found myself trying to explain the contemplative life, pointing out that praying is *not* doing nothing. Prayer is the greatest activity in the world. In fact, I was only doing what I hoped to do for all eternity — offer praise and adoration to God. But nothing I said could ever affect these people. As far as they were concerned, I was just a breathing lump, a parasite clinging to the side of Holy Mother Church — and one whose feet were probably cold. Then came my assignment to teach.

To say that I taught is a gross overstatement. That year when the course of studies was drawn up, it was evident to all that I had come out on the tail end of the curriculum — two hours a week. All mine, either because my superiors did not know what to do with the two hours, or because they did not know what to do with me. There was only one good thing about it. Now

I was able to tell the world that I taught, thereby side-stepping reams of futile explanations.

Well, for one hour on Friday and one hour on Saturday, I walked into a classroom and looked into the brilliant, vibrant, and intelligent eyes of theologians. I never even tried to fool them. I just settled down at my desk and spread my notes out before me. *I thought they were good notes.* I liked them because I had spent many hours drawing them up. Yet, I knew very well that in a mental joust, these boys could go through my notes like a snowplow. But I was their teacher.

I acquired a unique distinction there. I was perhaps the only homiletic professor in the history of the Church who got up before seminarians to tell them of the importance of distinct speech in effective pulpit work, and all the while, I slurred, jammed, elided, and smashed words. How I loved their charity as they sat there and took notes on my notes which I got from somebody else's notes. How I loved their simplicity as they sat there and listened to lectures on material that they had probably received by divine infusion many years ago.

There was some consolation in the work of teaching. I taught in a classroom because, for some fantastic reason, God wanted me there. And it was also gratifying to know that as a teacher, however stunted my knowledge might have been, it became with this a shared knowledge. It meant that there would always be a little bit of me in all the men I taught. And whenever they would go to do God's work later on, I would, in a way, go with them. This was the way I felt about it. How they felt, I do not know. I never asked.

Being a teacher has given me, if nothing else, a deeper appreciation of those who have completely dedicated their lives to the education of American and world youth. There are Teaching Brothers in classrooms around America today who, as far as intellectual requirements go, could be ordained priests tomorrow. But they have freely deprived themselves of any sacerdotal dignity so that nothing may distract them from their work of education. Sometimes, they make us ashamed of ourselves.

As for the Sisters who teach in our schools, what could be said that might befit them? How well they have fulfilled the command of Christ to "go and teach." They have *gone* by giving up the world for God. Now they *teach* in His name and for His glory. We shall never fully appreciate them or the effectiveness of their work. They probably do not understand it themselves. For it is never easy on a Sister to go into a classroom each morning, spend the day with a gang of "little animals," and then go home at night conscious that the only emotion she evoked from her pupils was the hope that, "maybe Sister will break her leg on the way home and we won't have school tomorrow." It's a tough world.

So in view of the fact that we have not appreciated teachers during life, we should offer them some fitting salute after death. We could pray for them. We could keep their memorial card in our breviary. But more than that, we could go from grave to grave and gently lay upon the fresh-turned soil a little plaque upon which could be engraved: "Here rests in peace and long-awaited slumber a teacher, whose soul has gone to God, but whose body has turned to chalk dust."

The Plague of the Pulpit

THIS chapter is being written at the beginning of Lent, and Lent among other things means that there will be weekly Lenten devotions in all parish churches. They will consist of Benediction, the Way of the Cross, and (horror of horrors) a sermon. Catholics who love God enough will attend these services, even though they *must* sit there and listen to a sermon.

No doubt about it, we priests pan off some very tedious preaching on our people. Some of us can rattle off the last words of Christ from His cross with about the same feeling that we would say "Please pass the butter." Or we can put as much hatred into a condemnation of sin as we would put into a condemnation of chocolate bars. But we try hard.

Why, however, must we use every trick in the book (and make up new ones) to make people listen to us? Whose fault is it? Conscious as we are of our short-comings, we still give the best possible preparation to our sermons. We have devoted much time to the reading of the Passion so that we might write down and later deliver a new slant on the Crucifixion for the benefit of our audience. We have given effort and plenty of it. So if and when our sermon fails, we wonder, is it all our

fault? Or does some of the blame rest with the people who sit out in the church, looking up at us.

People are a problem to the priest who preaches to them. They are the pivot of his success or failure. They give meaning to his words. It is true that Americans today are used to good speeches rendered through the medium of radio and TV. They deserve no less in their churches. But if we are not able to compete with the professionals, we beg our people to try at least to understand. People can criticize bad sermons, but if they had to climb into that pulpit, they would ask themselves the same questions that we priests do.

Why, for instance, does the large man with the shiny red face sit right beneath the pulpit and yawn through the whole sermon? (If we tumbled from our perch and fell into the gaping hole of his open mouth, we would never be found again.) Why do babies cry so long and so loud? Are they pinched for the sake of hastening our departure? Or if children are big enough to walk, why are they permitted to stand in the pews during the sermon and shout, "Come on, Mom. Let's go home"? Are they just fresh, or have they been prompted? Why do people blow their noses so endlessly and so resonantly? And when someone comes in late, why must people turn their heads to give far greater attention to the sluggard than they have been giving to the preacher? Why must they sit in the rear of the church and complain because they cannot hear us? How can we possibly cope with the Center Street trolley that barrels by the front door every eight minutes? Then, when the sermon is over, why do they come in and tell us they enjoyed it? They didn't even hear it. (Maybe that is the reason why they *did* enjoy it.)

All we ask of our people is that they be tolerant of us and charitable with their attention. If through our sermons we cannot make them love God more, then we have failed. For which we are deeply grieved. But no one should ever forget that God can use blunt chisels to carve beauty into a soul. That is our one consolation as we live each day with our bluntness.

Ordinarily, people do not realize what it takes to prepare and deliver a twenty-minute sermon. We do not just go up into the pulpit and talk (even though it might sound like it). Preaching is a tough, heartbreaking business. It is time-consuming work that takes first place on our agenda. Personally, I would say that it takes an entire week to prepare for a Lenten sermon that I might give on a Friday night. And when one sermon is sealed and delivered, I begin on the next one. All week I read and think. By the time Wednesday comes around, I have a sheaf of notes. Then on Friday morning, I begin the long, arduous task of learning the sermon. Most of us do this because we know that people do not like to have sermons read to them. So if nothing else, when we priests go into the pulpit, we do not carry any papers.

And speaking in conversation is one thing; speaking from a pulpit is another. Preaching takes the consistent working of teeth, tongue, lips, and jaw. If we give our full attention to this, then we are prone to forget where our hands are. And if we try to track down the aimless wanderings of our gestures, then we might easily forget what we want to say.

So we have our troubles. Still, they do not stop us from preaching to our people. In fact, we will talk about Christ anywhere, any time, to anyone who will listen. We want to make Christ real in men's minds and imaginations. But we are such dubbers.

When I became a priest, the Church did not say to me, "Preach if you are able." She just said, "Preach." So my fellow priests and I preach. If our people do not enjoy our sermons, let them try to listen anyway. The blessing of God falls upon those who place themselves on the receiving end of a sermon. So if they will not come for the words, let them at least come for the grace.

❧ XXVI ❧

God's Little Women

THEY overrun conventions and crowd summer schools. They turn out *en masse* for a benefactor's funeral. They are artists, dramatists, sculptors, musicians, scientists, and saints — often all rolled into one. They convert pagans, educate children, mother orphans, run hospitals, and coddle priests. They probably do more work, person for person, than anybody else in the Church. They are never called nuns unless the word "holy" is prefixed to their title. They are simply referred to as "Sisters."

Most of us priests have had frequent contact with the Sisters. We have said Mass in their convents. We have been their confessors and spiritual directors. We have been their retreat masters. Yet, we have never given them more than they have given us.

We could, for the sake of convenience, divide Sisters into two groups: those who are entirely contemplative and those who are not. Basically, however, they are the same. They do not glide along on wheeled shoes; they really walk. Their habits may not make them look like women; but they are. And what is most difficult to believe about them is that they were once girls like all other girls. They enjoyed living (they still do). They sang (they still do). They sipped soda and cokes (they still do). They danced at high school proms (but no more). If they are tickled, they laugh; if they are cut, they bleed. They are rational, intelligent beings who think and breathe. Sometimes they make mistakes. But we dread to think of what might happen to the Church if they stopped being — like the poor — always with us.

More often talked about than seen, are the contemplative nuns. What are *they* like? The most we can say about them is that they have become to the world like "the strange friends and friendly strangers." For their life stands in complete contradiction to modern living. They have given the lie to the present-day maxim of "take care of yourself; nobody else matters." They have injected shame into the veins of luxury. They have silenced by their own silence the blasphemies of the mobs, they have conquered by their own humility the advocates of concupiscence and pride. They have done all this, not directly, for that is not the primary end of their vocations. But by bringing men closer to God, they have made evil less functional. They have put sin on crutches.

Taking their life at its face value, I do not think that they, in a certain sense, really enjoy it. I am rather sure that they do not get a tremendous kick out of austerity. They certainly have no personal emnity toward a steak or a hamburger. Undoubtedly they wonder, at times, what has changed on the other side of their all embracing walls, what their home town looks like with the new courthouse in the city square, and the new-fangled parking meters on Main Street. They probably wonder what it feels like to ride in an airplane, play a jukebox, or watch a television program.

Standing beside human strength, they are weak. But it is their very weakness that has made them so strong. It is their very segregation from the world that has brought the world panting to their door. Who else could make loud-mouthed men whisper in passing a convent? Who else could make unbelievers stop for a moment outside their walls and mutter, "I don't understand it but they sure have *something*." Only they could do it for they have sold contemplation to the world without the world's even knowing it. And just as skin is grafted from one member to the other, so they have grafted the good from their own lives to the souls of others. And the thing that gives them the most joy is to know the people, whom they shall never see, are dropping into their chapels to pray with them.

As for those who are not absolutely contemplative, they have shown themselves extraordinarily resourceful in the face of great odds. They have not only spent their time with children; they have, through the children, infiltrated themselves into careless Catholic homes. Their system is foolproof. A little seven-year-old comes home from school and says, "Hey, Pop, Sister says that this is Holy Name Sunday and you have to get to confession Saturday night." Then on Sunday morning the kid is at his father's bedside screaming, "Come on, Pop, get up. Sister says you have to be on time for the seven." Then on Sunday evening the child goes to work again, "Pop, Sister says we should say the rosary together." What can "Pop" do? So Sister says this and Sister says that and the whole world picks itself up a bit.

Yes, through the mouths of children, they have

brought Christ into Catholic homes in a way that many of us would have never thought possible. Parents have put their wild, bawling children into their hands and said, "Educate them. Teach them something. Make something out of them." And they have. They have educated not only the minds of the children. They have educated their hearts and their souls. The Sisters have seen in children the pulse of a nation and they have put their hand upon it and guided it. And because our present adult generation has failed, in great part, to carry high the torch of faith, the Sisters have gone to the children. That is why, if the world is better twenty years from now (and it will be) it is the Sisters who will be largely responsible for it. It is they who will deserve the praise. But they won't hear any of it. They will be in their classrooms still at it, making things even better.

We priests, as well as all Catholics, owe an infinite debt to the Sisters for their unstinted, unglamorous work in the schools, the hospitals, the institutions, and the missions. They have never failed us. And if a man knows no more about his faith than that he should tip his hat to a priest, it was probably a Sister who told him about it. They reach the little and the great, the poor and the rich. They have filled every need in a way that is without equal in the history of the Church.

They face criticism many times. On occasions they are belittled. But if tomorrow, one hundred and forty thousand Sisters died, we, with all our powers of the priesthood, would be strongly tempted to sit down in all frustration and despair and say, "That does it. This is the end."

☞ XXVII ☜

Just Kids

A POSITION on the faculty of a minor seminary is no job for a priest who does not like kids (if there is such a priest). It changes the whole tenor of his life. It takes him out of the pulpit and puts him into the study hall. Instead of writing sermons, he writes conferences. And instead of developing a strong mind, he develops a strong arm. He loses his perspective, he loses his head, he loses a lot of weight. He awakens them in the morning, takes them to chapel, eats with them, teaches them, supervises their study periods, plays ball, skis or swims with them, heals their many wounds, and puts them to bed at night with the sign of the cross.

This was my life for two years. So it is not hard to understand why all of us priests in the seminary breathed a sigh of weary relief when the end of the year came around. In the early part of June the seminary closed down for the summer and in a flurry of excited youth, the boys began their journey home. It was a wonderful day for them. It meant a temporary reprieve from the long, arduous journey to the altar. It meant reunion with the families that they had given up for the unmatched service of almighty God.

As was customary, a few of us priests went along with

the boys to the depot to see that they climbed aboard the right trains. Then, with a final blessing, we waved good-by through the windows of the moving coaches, and returned home to begin preparations for the following year.

As we rode home we thought of our own days in the seminary when we had gone home and left the priests by the railroad tracks, wrapped in the swirling steam of a departing train. We thought of the changelessness of the years, with things happening today just as they had happened fifteen years ago. The same kinds of boys going home and looking like Ichabod Cranes in suits that they had remarkably outgrown. The same kinds of boys with the same kind of luggage, and with the same happy lilt to their voices as they slapped farewells on the backs of one another. Those were the carefree days when even hunger was stifled by happy apprehension. Yes, we thought about these things. For us those days were over. But for us there was still the job to see that these things never ended, that there would always be boys to send home in the spring and welcome back again in the fall. It was our sacred duty to see that the dreams of young men for a sacerdotal dignity always remained strong and real. It was our duty to help and encourage them, to make up to them in some way for the things they had sacrificed.

On the way back to the seminary and all through the summer, we thought long hard thoughts about our work. We checked on our past mistakes and determined why some things went wrong and how they could be righted. And while we thought these things, we would swell with pride over the fact that there were still boys, high school boys of every age, who even today possessed the courage and the fearlessness of mature men.

For to many, these boys are a puzzle. The world says that they do not know their own mind. The world says that they are too young to make decisions that will affect their whole life. The world cries out to them to wait and taste the emptiness that it has to offer them. It wants them to gamble their vocation against its own futility. It wants them to wait and cultivate their call from God in environments that are often anything *but* conducive to the cultivation of a vocation.

This is exactly why, when a boy just out of grammar school enters a minor seminary, everyone but himself thinks he is blind and foolish. Everyone suffers and feels his loss; everyone, that is, except himself. Certainly we cannot say that *all* boys who want to become priests must enter a minor seminary. But for those who *do* enter at an early age, we can only say that when a fourteen-year-old boy leaves home to enter a seminary, he *does* know what he wants. True, he does not know the whole story of life, sordid as it is sometimes; but he does know that he wants to be a priest. That is why he goes. He might still be in that age bracket where he cannot, for the life of him, understand why God even bothered to make girls. He may not understand the deadly pull of wealth or the long, devious caverns through which money can lead him. He may not feel the deadly touch of pride or see the grim shadow of worldly glory across his path. But the dreams he holds of a priest upon the altar are to him valid enough reason for his scurry to the seminary. All these things of the world he will see and meet as he grows. And as he grows, he will receive the corresponding lights to choose what he wants.

But the greatest factor entering into the life of a minor seminarian is the oft-spoken but rarely understood "grace of God." It is the grace of God that makes a fourteen-year-old boy find high adventure in leaving for the seminary. It is the same grace of God that makes him grow up in a seminary, not in ignorance of the world he rides above; but in clear penetration of what he wants to do with his life. It is, too, the grace of God which preordains a child for the holy priesthood.

The answer to God's call is never fulfilled by deferred decisions. It is not strengthened by rubbing shoulders with the "uncalled." It is something that lies deeply within a boy's heart, and only he and God can see into that depth. Only he and God can understand the reason for what he does.

And so each June, into their bags they pack worn-out clothing and a weird assortment of all kinds of knick-knacks which they have, to the complete amazement of seminary authorities, picked up during their year's residence at school. Then they say good-by to one another and go home to their individual problems, and to the grating, trying, baffling clichés of their friends: "You are so young. You just don't know. . . ."

But they know. They are quite old enough to see, in the salvation of souls, the greatest, most imperative, most needed work of their generation. They are quite old enough to see that the world is a nice place, and people are nice, but that these things are not for them. They are not disillusioned. They are not hoaxed. They are not ignorant children. For in their choice and in their decision, they have attained full maturity. And the only reason why they are not priests today is that they were not born ten years earlier.

❧ XXVIII ❧

Come Aside and Rest

WE FRIARS are better off in our monastery. Behind our secure walls, we need not be afraid of sinning against the social graces. We need not suffer shame at our ignorance of current events. We need not worry about burning holes in fine upholstery, or putting our feet on the rich sheen of a Chinese teakwood table, or balancing a demi-tasse on our knee. If we forget to shave in the morning, we can get away with it till after breakfast. If we break a dish, we kiss the floor and forget about it. We are not bound to a Hoyle or a Post. We can be odd, different, unusual, unique — blooming nitwits, in fact, but as long as we attend community exercises and do what we should, we are safe.

However, once in a while this complacency is demolished. We find ourselves leaving the Prior's room with traveling expenses, an address in some city, and a command, "Give this retreat." We pack slowly, travel casually to the depot, and because we think the world will wait for us, we find ourselves streaking like a gazelle after a departing train and swinging ourselves into the rear door of the last car, while a Negro porter smiles and says, "Man, that is runnin'."

If we are scheduled for a convent and if we are still

young priests (under fifty) the first problem is to get into the place. If we have been in religious life only fifteen years, we are not supposed to know anything; we must only stand there before the withering gaze of Mother Superior while she mentally anathematizes those Priors who do not send older priests (over fifty) to give them their retreats.

The first conference is always the critical one. You walk out on the altar to say the introductory prayers. Most retreatants do not put much heart into the first prayer. They are too busy looking you over. They check your over-all height and weight, the size of your feet, and the shape of your head. They watch whether you shuffle out like a bear or dance out like a sprite. Satisfied at last that you are not one of the three-headed kind, they sit back and wait for you to open your mouth.

The priest says to himself, "Well, here I am. Whether you like it or not, I am here to give this retreat. I give it because you need it. You are good people, perhaps, but not good enough. You are saints, perhaps, but not saintly enough. I am going to put the faults of your life up before your eyes where you cannot possibly avoid them. And I will challenge you to deny their existence. Beyond this, I will encourage you to do better. I will praise you, in fact, for the good that you possess. And when I leave here, I will expect you to have changed; not through any efforts of my own, but through the grace of God that will be with you during the retreat."

And while the priest is clearing his throat preparatory to his first words, the retreatants are saying to themselves, "All right, Father, you're a priest. You're supposed to know all the answers. Give them to us. Change us if you can. Destroy our attachments if you can. Tell us about God. Tell us about His mercy; give us faith to see the reason for our existence. Make us saints if you can. We dare you."

So the flag comes down and the battle is on. The priest begins to speak; the retreatants begin to listen.

As far as profiting souls goes, the retreat is a perfect setup. It offers an atmosphere entirely conducive to growth in perfection. Through its silence and its pointedness it forces people to look at themselves as they really are and not as they seem to think they are. They become receptive and interested. They are ready to be led. And any priest may find in this kind of work the most perfect outlet for his ardor and his zeal.

A priest does not have to use any beautiful words to get the important points across. He does not have to render a deep, scholarly treatment of the great truths of faith. He does not have to present anything new (only the old truths in dressed-up façades). Everything he says carries an added force. He could say to some man on a bus, "God made you from nothing. He made you for one reason, to live and be happy with Him for all eternity in heaven." Say this to a man on a bus and it doesn't make much of an impression. But say the same thing to the same man in the seclusion of a closed retreat, and it rocks him back on his heels. He is forced to say to himself, "If God made me, then I was the direct object of His divine power. If He made me from nothing, then to Him I owe my existence. And if He made me for heaven, then why am I fooling around here on earth? Why am I not working to achieve what God wants me to achieve — a share in His heaven." Get a man to think like this long enough, and he becomes a different man. Make him a different man and evil loses points.

Retreats can be short or long. The short one can be a delight; the long one, however, can sometimes become a little tedious. We priests who give retreats know this. It is not always an easy job. We think hard all day long. We speak often. We advise hour after hour. When we hear confessions, we sit in the darkness waiting for the end of the line that is never there. And when, at day's end, we think that if one more person comes in the box, we will scream. But they come in; and we don't scream. We welcome them in God's name.

Yet, the hard part is negligible in the face of the good that comes out of it. So, when we go out to give a retreat, we are glad to do it. It is not rest for the priest who gives it; but it might easily be a rest for the person who submits to it. After all, the words of Christ apply to the retreatants. To each one of them, He says, "Come aside a while and rest." And thank God for the chance.

※XXIX※

Not Even the Angels

ALMOST every morning of the year about forty thousand of us American men (who are lovingly referred to as "Father" by their people) walk humbly into our sacristies and clothe ourselves in the sacred vestments. Then getting squared away with an acolyte, we take our chalice into our hands and advance upon the altar to do that which is not even given to angels. We begin the celebration of Mass. And as we do, I suppose even *we* do not get the full wonder of what we do. As for the people who kneel in the pews watching us, they gaze at our movements with uncomprehending eyes.

It is unfortunate that the Sacrifice of the Mass is so little understood. The over-all picture of Catholics hearing Mass is pretty much the same everywhere. They are there, slumped in the pew, either whirling rosary beads around their fingers or paging through some inadequate prayer book. Some cling tenaciously (and uncharitably) to the seat on the aisle and demand that everyone else climb awkwardly over them. Many others, however, manage to squeeze into the pews at the back of the church, where they can more easily make an unretarded escape toward the end of Mass. To these and many like them, Mass is nothing more than a priest executing a series of intricate maneuvers with a couple of little altar boys crisscrossing around him with a big red book and a pair of cruets.

Yet, upon the altar, almighty God is physically present. Calvary is being continued. Christ is still mystically shedding His Blood. And grief of all griefs, sorrow of all sorrows, people are bored!

However, the faithful take a more intimate part in the Mass than they sometimes realize. Certainly we priests are conscious of this supporting role of the faithful when we go out to the altar, stand at the bottom step and confess our great unworthiness before God. We count on their assistance as we ascend the steps to begin Mass. Consistently, we use the plural to speak to God. Several times during Mass we turn to implore their help and their co-operation. All of us together go through that Mass and arrive ultimately to the great moment, the Consecration.

I think I can speak for all priests when I say that never do we feel so small as when we take the host into our hands and breathe words of life into it. There are occasions when we feel like giants — when we stand up before the world to preach the word of God, or carry the torch of faith through the darkness of our age. We feel big when we realize that common opinion has acknowledged us as one of the most educated, penetrating, calculating groups of men on the face of the earth. But when we stand over that host and pronounce the words of consecration, we become as midgets before the wonder of God's love. Our world is full of miracles, but none nearly so great as this.

We do it each day. And the more we do it, the less we are able to grasp the extent of it all. For example, taking the words out of their context, we say. "For this is *my* Body." We use the word *my* knowing that it is not *our* Body. It is the Body of Christ. And if it *is* the body of Christ, then it must be Christ who lays claim to His own body. And if Christ is there claiming His own body, then what happens to us? Where have we gone? What has become of us? Could it be that at the consecration the priest isn't there any more — just Christ? We continue to be *other* Christs, giving Him other humanities in which He may perform this tremendous miracle every morning. Thoughts like this make us stumble. They make us stop and wonder. . . .

But in spite of all the things we do not understand, because we are finite and unable to plumb the depths of infinite mystery, there are some things of which we are certain. We know that, as priests upon the altar, representing all men, we become intercessors between heaven and earth. We become the bridge that spans the gap between God and man. We become mediators, taking the prayers of all creatures to the feet of God, then returning to earth with the treasures of Eternal Goodness. We do this for our people and nothing else could give us greater joy. Nothing else could make our lives as rich or our vocations as precious.

This alone is sufficient for our existence as priests. If we did nothing else with our lives but say Mass each morning, the world would still be the better for our efforts. It is our life to offer sacrifice, the one great Sacrifice. Through this we are able, in the person of all the faithful, to give to God the most perfect, infallible measure of praise and adoration. It is an adoration that is completely worthy of God. And for weak human beings to do this — this is the wonder and the power of the Mass.

Not even the angels can do it. But we can. Each morning of our life we touch and taste Christ. We meet Him in a way that should not be given to mortal men. Yet, God not only permits it. He demands it. He has shared with us to the highest possible degree His own Godhead. Small wonder that we cannot live and act as other men.

Simeon lived a long, long life before he sang his "Nunc dimittis." He held Christ once, which left him with nothing else to live for. So he died. But we priests do not hold Christ only once. We held Him this morning and we did not die. We will live to do it again tomorrow and, please God, many tomorrows to come. We live on to say to men, "I will remember you in my Mass." And when we do, when we finish the Sacrifice, we come into the sacristy, bless the acolyte and kneel down before the prayer card to say, "Look down upon me, good and gentle Jesus." But we do not get far before we start asking ourselves the great questions, "Why did God leave us the Mass?" and even more, "Why did He create me to offer it?" There is no answer to this. There is none necessary; there is none possible. All we can do is to love Christ even more and to get back to our prayers on the sacristy wall, "Look down upon me, good and gentle Jesus, while before Thy face I humbly kneel. . . ."

❧ XXX ❧

Our Shared Vocation

THESE pages have been written with a hope that the ultimate result of the whole thing will stand as some contribution to the cause of religious vocations. Whatever else it might be, it is the story of one vocation anyway. It has been undertaken with a prayer that through these pages, youth will see even more clearly that to be a priest in our own times can easily be one of the most thrilling experiences in the world. Just as long as we take care that "thrill" be removed from all emotional entanglements. It is said that the fullness of happiness rests in the fulfillment of all desires. And if a man becomes a priest, what is left to be desired? Can a priest seek any more save heaven itself? In this realization rests the happiness that we find in the service of God.

So we appreciate the fruition of our vocation. But it would be the height of presumption on our part to imagine, for even one moment, that we have become religious of ourselves. Our vocations are not independent, isolated things. Our vocations found fulfillment only through another vocation — the vocation of our mothers and fathers. We, as the fruits of their love, have been able to become what we are. To speak of their vocation as a half vocation, something secondary, given only to those who were not good enough to be religious, would be to minimize the wisdom of God and to belittle our own life.

We have been able to offer ourselves to God only because our parents gave us life in the first place. And this, indeed, is no small thing. To die is no problem. The problem is to *live*. And personally, I dread to think of my eternal frustration, if knowing in some vague, mysterious, nonexistent way, that God had destined me from all eternity to be a priest; and yet, I was never lucky enough to get myself born. Some kids never make it. And of these kids who never did make it, certainly many of them could have been and would have been priests. But they never received hands upon which could be traced the oils of ordination, they never received feet upon which they might walk in the footprints of Christ, they never even lived. It is true that our vocation is a divine gift, but it hinged precariously upon the free will of our parents. Therefore, it is to our parents that we priests owe our ability to live our lives as we desire to lead them and as God demands we lead them.

Further, we owe our vocations to the generosity of our parents who willingly waved good-by to us as we entrained for distant seminaries or monasteries. This is no small thing either. Certainly it is a crying shame that so many vocations are lost through parental objection. We can understand the attitude of such parents but we cannot condone it. For they make a very apparent mistake in thinking that they can see farther than

God. They fall into error by projecting their own mentality into the mentality of their children by saying, "I could never have found happiness in religious life, so neither could our children." They labor under some sort of delusion which tells them that the essence of happiness rests in "Making good in the world" (which is just another set of lyrics for the old "get rich" song). We can only sympathize with such parents while our hearts break for the children who must sacrifice their vocations at the altar of distorted parental ideas.

With such thinking more than rarely prevalent in our times, blessed is the child who finds his parents heart and soul behind him in his desire to become a priest. We who have had such parents have found in them one of our greatest incentives to carry on in spite of the many difficulties encountered in the course of priestly training. At the cost of some loneliness on their part, at the price of separation, they have joined with us in the accomplishment of our highest hopes. So they understood, as they knelt for the first blessing of their sons, why God brought them together. They understood their own vocation and they exalted in it.

So, obviously, parents play a great part in the fostering and development of a child's vocation. And maybe before Christ looks into the heart of a boy, He looks first into the hearts of his parents. He looks into the homes. And if we could speak of Christ as going around looking for vocations in Catholic homes, we wonder what He would think of the things He saw. In some homes He would be painfully aware of the absence of anything that would bear witness to the faith. No crucifix on the wall, no image of His Sacred Heart to proclaim Him as King of the household. He would see staggered portraits on the walls, and flying geese (all very proper and in good taste, of course) but no crucifix, no statue. From such homes as these Christ might easily turn. And in turning from them in His quest for followers, He might more easily take up His stand in the home where He finds parents leading the rosary for their children each night, teaching them their prayers, building pride in their faith. Yes, Christ might surely do His recruiting in such homes as these. He might easily drop the germ of a vocation in the home of a young dentist with four beautiful children and one on the way, who says, "Father, to what degree may I provide for my family until I can take literally the words of Christ, 'Go, sell what thou hast and give to the poor.'" And He might pause for serious consideration at the side of the young mother of nine children who says, "I love my family. With all these, I have a better chance of becoming the mother of a priest." Yes, these are the homes where Christ shall pause to rest and to bless. Among such people as these He knows that His gift of vocation will be cherished and revered.

So before we religious take bows for any glory that has come into our lives as the result of our vocations, we should remember that such glory must be a shared thing. And our parents must get a great part of it. They have spent years raising a family, struggling sometimes against great odds, giving themselves hour by hour, never seeking praise, never wanting any. They have freely given their children to God, heedless of who should provide for their old age, resigned completely to

His will, settled entirely within the harbor of His Divine Providence.

As for those parents whose prayers for a vocation among their children have apparently gone unanswered, let them never forget that, even though their children, or their children's children never received a vocation, they still might be responsible, however remotely, for the ascent of some boy to the altar of God in the far distant future.

When those of us who are priests come to the end of our lives as shepherds of souls, we might honestly ask ourselves, "Whose life was more heroic, whose life was more brim-filled with sacrifice, ours or our parents? And being true to ourselves we might be forced to admit that we never knew the meaning of sacrifice as our parents knew it. We never knew worry as they knew it. And although we followed Christ on His way up Calvary, we probably never tasted the intensity of His suffering nearly as much as those two, who in highest dignity and in closest partnership with God, gave us life and with that the chance to become a priest.

We must work for our salvation as they must work. Our salvation depends on the depth of our zeal for souls. But to those who have given themselves to God, and their children to the church, surely someday they will find a place beside Him of whom it was said, "And of His kingdom, there shall be no end." 4/15/56